DIARY FROM A
SOUTH AFRICAN PRISON

TSHENUWANI SIMON FARISANI

Edited by John A. Evenson

Fortress Press   **Philadelphia**

Biblical quotations are from the Authorized King James Version of the Holy Bible.

Library of Congress Cataloging-in-Publication Data

Farisani, T. Simon (Tshenuwani Simon)
Diary from a South African prison.

1. Farisani, T. Simon (Tshenuwani Simon)
2. Political prisoners—South Africa—Biography.
3. Apartheid—South Africa. I. Title.
HV9850.5.A26 1987   365'.45'0924 [B]   87-45317
ISBN 0-8006-2062-3

3004E87 Printed in the United States of America 1-2062

CONTENTS

MESSAGE TO
THE READER

TSHENUWANI SIMON FARISANI

Before and after Steve Biko, many have died in detention. According to police reports, they have died by slipping on a piece of soap in the shower, by suicide, by accidentally banging their heads against the wall, or by heart attack. Others are said to have jumped out of the tenth-floor window of the John Vorster Square Prison, to have drowned in the toilet, or to have sustained injuries in resisting arrest.

Have we heard the full story? Is this the way Timol, Mohapi, Biko, Aggett, Muofhe, Nchabeleng, and the many others have met their end? I am personally waiting to hear another version on Judgment Day! Most magistrates and judges accept the police version as the gospel truth and almost always return the verdict "Nobody can be held responsible for the detainee's death. . . . There is no reason to reject the police evidence that the detainee took his own life."

Overwhelming evidence of torture has been amassed by former detainees and by trialists,* by the church, and by political, lawyers', medical, and other human-rights groups. All of this, however, is routinely brushed aside by the South African government and judiciary as "communist propaganda, an evil crusade, a total onslaught to discredit and destabilize our good government, our Christian society, democracy, Western civilization, and the capitalist economy." "This campaign," the defenders of the status quo argue, "is waged by terrorists and murderers masquerading as suave gentlemen and women, by faceless spiritual witch doctors in clerical garb." And so the government continues to pay out-

---

*In South Africa, "trialists" refers to people on trial in the courts for political reasons.

of-court settlements without in any way compromising the innocence of the police, whose conduct is always aboveboard. (Of course, this same government sees no contradiction in "separate, parallel, but equal development.") They willingly paid me out of court—along with two other pastors—for a "slight headache" that kept me in the hospital for 106 days in 1982, during my third detention.

After my second detention, Bishop Serote and I, on behalf of our church council, met the minister of justice in Cape Town to protest detention and torture in general, and mine in particular. We deliberately avoided "cheap publicity," hoping that our "responsible" way of protest would bear fruit. He promised to look into the matter. Police harassments continued, and deaths in detention. I was denied a passport to attend church meetings in Europe. As a reward, I have since landed twice in detention. South African–style dialogue! As I write, the minister is still looking into our matter, as Pharaoh looked into Moses' matter. I hope that my story has not, as in Biko's case, "left him cold." Now I have decided to go public, in spite of the probable consequences!

In one small sense this is a personal story, but in another wider, more realistic sense it is South Africa's tragic story. I do not aim at discrediting the already hopelessly discredited white racist regime, their surrogates, or their security apparatus. I do not wish to retaliate against my black and white torturers. It is not my intention to create a martyr out of one who spent only 442 days in four detentions. Many others have been held longer. The Mandelas and Sisulus are in for life. I have seen Robben Island only from the comfort of Table Mountain. This is our experience: our oppression, our torture, our suffering. Our death. Our hope. Our inevitable victory. Our freedom.

I have taken the risk of telling the story, first to groups, then in the videofilm *The Torture of a South African Pastor*, and now in the black and white of print. The police have warned me not to do this. I am telling the story not because of courage nor out of the desire to embarrass the gods of oppression and the angels of hell. How I wish I could tell a different story about the country I love so much, whose citizens are both black and white!

Do you find my story difficult to believe? So do I. Will the average white mother accept this ugly truth? Had my mother not seen me lying wounded in hospital, she would find it difficult to believe. Will the government and police believe me? "Next time we get him . . . " Do I have witnesses? Plenty. Many of them are dumb: police, guards or warders, magistrates, attorneys, doctors, nurses, radiographers, former fellow detainees, fellow patients, those who saw me "by accident," those who visited me at Tshilidzini hospital, black and white, pastors, deans, bishops, lecturers, members of the International Red Cross, and my family. On Judgment Day, thirteen police cells, the "truth rooms," eleven police stations and prisons, handcuffs, leg irons, liberation sticks and brooms, chairs, electric gadgets, and many other unwilling instruments of torture will willingly come forward to testify. On this day, many verdicts of "Nobody can be held responsible. . . . " will be reversed by the Impartial Judge before whom no judge who has passed an honorable verdict to dishonor all that is true, all that is good, all that is just, and all that is humane, will escape.

To whom shall I dedicate this book? To the security police and the white regime, the main actors of the drama? To the prophetic bishops Scharf, Kruse, and Propst Hollm? To Hanna Lechler Steffens, that indomitable prophetess, and her husband, Wilhelm, and children? To a friend in need who is a friend indeed, the Reverend John Evenson, and his family? To Amnesty International or the International Red Cross? To Bishop Tutu, Beyers Naude, Allan Boesak, and the SACC? To my own church and its leaders? To human-rights groups in South Africa and on other continents? To MWASA, the Media Workers Association of South Africa? To attorneys and advocates Jana, Krish, Naidoo, Don Nkadimeng, and Mohammed? To governments and embassies that cared? To the Lutheran World Federation? To my parents, Ratshilumela and Musandiwa, who watched in love and helplessness and tears every time the mighty tore me away for months? To Regina Mudzunga, my loving, caring, and praying partner, without whom I would either be a complete spiritual wreck or a pale statistic in the casualty lists of Amnesty International and our own Detainees' Parents Support Committee? To our children, Nzumbu, Ndamu, and Zwo, who have gone through the school of fatherlessness and learned to pray, "Father God, be with us and protect us tonight because the police have taken our father. Don't let the police beat our father again. . . . " To our friends and relatives? To the Confessing Fellowship? To the churches in the United States, Europe, Africa, Canada, Asia, and elsewhere?

I know that the people and groups mentioned will not accept my offer. Not even my spiritual father, Dean Patrick Masupye Masekela, whose sudden death on January 28, 1987—two days before my release from the fourth detention—can be safely attributed to exhaustion and sleepless nights, as the seventy-three-year-old diabetic and disciple of Christ fasted and labored day and night for my release. On January 30, 1987, Judith, his elderly widow, threw sorrow and traditional rites to the wind, walked to my house, collapsed on me, and sobbed in joy, "Your father

Masekela is no more. He has died for you. He is gone, but thank God you are back. Why has God not spared him to see you free? Thank God Farisani is free! Are you back, Tshenuwani my son?" I embraced her, lame, sobbing. Rainbow rays lined every drop of her tears. I broke down and wept, my tears mixed with hers. Everyone in the room joined. We could hear Jesus say, "Behold your son . . . behold your mother . . ." (John 19:26–27).

This book is dedicated to God's unfailing program, to the hope that we hold for justice and freedom in South Africa and the world over. It is dedicated to that day when Pretoria-style widows, Winnie Mandela and all like her, shall embrace their resurrected loved ones and say, "Many have since died. . . . Why has God not . . .? Thank God you are free."

St. Paul, Minnesota
April 21, 1987

INTRODUCTION

JOHN A. EVENSON

South Africa. Images spring to the minds of Westerners: police wielding the harsh whips known as sjamboks, rhythmically descending on the bodies of black youths . . . angry young men and weeping mothers as yet another funeral of the young occurs in the black townships . . . Western leaders protesting that they do, indeed, "abhor apartheid, but . . ." . . . business men, telling of all the good they have done . . . while the foundation of white minority rule remains firmly in place and thousands continue to be imprisoned without trial. P. W. Botha warns the world, "We are not weak." Archbishop Desmond Tutu speaks yet again in hope of peaceful change. We see a twenty-five-year-old picture of Nelson Mandela, the imprisoned black leader whose presence is powerfully felt throughout South Africa and the world. These are the images we remember, images from afar, chosen for our consumption by the reporters and editors of the Western media.

Life in southern Africa is best described by those who live it. But the firsthand report from the black people of South Africa is often missing. This book by the Reverend Dr. Tshenuwani Simon Farisani is such a witness. Unfiltered by Western preconceptions and justifications, this is the personal account of the struggle of a pastor and prophet for truth in a land that mocks all concepts of justice. It is a witness that must be heard if one is to begin to understand the depth of evil that permeates the minority-rule system of South Africa today.

John A. Evenson is Director of the Namibian Christian Communications Trust in London.

11

In the international community, many have come face to face with Dean Simon Farisani, deputy bishop of the Evangelical Lutheran Church in Southern Africa, in his work with the wider church, his extensive preaching abroad, or his tireless efforts to assist the work of Amnesty International. Clearly those who have heard him in person or seen him in the film *The Torture of a South African Pastor* know him to be a person of deep faith, of strong courage, and of almost boundless forgiveness. The personal story in this book of his first three detentions by South Africa's security police is an important witness, a powerful indictment of those who think that simple cosmetic reforms, without permitting true self-determination, will be enough to solve the problems of that troubled land. (A short epilogue informs the reader of Farisani's situation up to the time of the book's publication.)

Tshenuwani Farisani was born in 1947, one year before the elections that brought South Africa's present government into power. Tshenuwani was born in the northern Transvaal, the extreme northeast corner of what is now the Republic of South Africa. Tshenu's ancestors had lived in the area for centuries, farming and grazing their cattle on the rich, fertile land. The Afrikaners, Europeans of primarily Dutch heritage, trekked from the south into the Transvaal in the early nineteenth century. At first they were few, and an uneasy truce prevailed between the "Boers" and the Africans already in place, the Venda, Sotho, and Shangan peoples. Then, as now, the white "pioneers" were vying for the rich, well-watered earth.

The Christian missionaries arrived in this area in the last third of the nineteenth century. The first, a Rev. Karl ("Pik") Beuster, came in 1872, sent by the Berlin Missionswerk. When more white settlers came, toward the end of the century, fierce battles took place over ownership of the land. The Boers, or farmers, brought reinforcements from the south with guns and cannon. With the aid of the European missionaries, who lived with the Africans and were able to pass on information to their white Christian brothers, the Boers triumphed. It is with justification, proved by official mission records from the period, that Africans complain that the whites brought them the Bible with one hand and, while they were at prayer, stole their land with the other.

Of course, white South African myths state that the land now reserved for whites was uninhabited before the Boers arrived. At the time most whites were convinced that Africans were less than human, so the myths have some basis in prejudiced "truth." But the belief endures to this day among many whites that blacks are subhuman, to be treated as chattel, or at best as perpetual children. Only the greater intellectual capacities of civilized Europeans, the myth continues, were able to utilize the riches of the soil.

This racist myth collapses when one hears the witness from the African people themselves. When Tshenu was born the family lived at Swongozwi, just above Louis Trichardt, then a small white city. Tshenu's father had already been expelled two times from more fertile areas as the whites designated more and more of the land as reserved for their use alone. At Swongozwi, the family had found an area where they could plant a large garden and an orchard. Because of the agricultural skills of his father, so much food was produced, and of such quality, that they were able to sell the surplus to white hotels and shops in Louis Trichardt.

But in 1951 the family was again subjected to forced removal to make way for whites. Their orchard and farm, it was claimed, were causing "soil erosion." Though only four years old at the time, Tshenu has never forgotten the experience of his hard-working family, his mother, his sisters and brothers, and his father's other wives, as they moved with the few possessions they were able to carry to the place designated for them by the white overseers. The family lost almost everything, and there was no compensation.

The new area was comparatively dry, and Tshenu's father could not farm as before. Being resourceful, he decided to specialize, and between 1951 and 1959 he built up a herd of about 140 cattle.

At the time, the government was building a road from Johannesburg to what was then Southern Rhodesia. The Africans have great respect for their ancestors, and Tshenu remembers the horror of seeing bulldozers rip through African grave sites. He remembers thinking that the gods of the whites were destroying his ancestors. Defiantly, Tshenu and the other boys would stone the bulldozers, and then flee into the bush.

Until Farisani was twelve, there were no schools or medical facilities available for blacks. The children were taught traditional skills, oral traditions passed on by his father, a traditional medicine man. In the religion of his ancestors, Tshenu learned that the world could be viewed as concentric circles. The Supreme Being encircles all and permeates through the inner rings, first the ancestors and the spirits, then humanity, then the animal kingdom and inanimate objects in the center. Thus the Supreme Being spoke through the spirits and ancestors. As a medicine man, Father Farisani was relied upon to protect the community. Tshenu was proud of his father.

While at this dwelling place, Tshenuwani's mother became very ill. Traditional medicine did not help. She was finally taken to a church hospital, but even after surgery she did not feel fully healed. After years of frustration, she met a woman who was a member of the Lutheran congregation, where prayers for healing were offered. She went to that church, and the healing long sought for took place. Tshenu's mother became a Christian and started to take her son with her to church. She is still alive today at seventy-five years of age, and works in the fields like a young woman.

In 1959 the family was again uprooted by the South African government. This time the family was forced to sell all their cattle and move to Mbabada, in a barren area under a chief known as Kutama. Suddenly the twelve-year-old Tshenu was part of a family with no cattle, no milk, no fields, no goats. They were reduced to begging, to looking after another family's cattle in the hope of getting a few drops of milk.

The move to Kutama had a disastrous effect on the family's fortunes. Tshenu's father was despondent, torn this time from any livelihood as a farmer. The one opportunity it did afford was for Tshenu, for now he was near a community school. There he was introduced to reading and writing, to morning prayer, and soon he was himself baptized. The heady mix of new faith and knowledge provided new hope for the gifted twelve-year-old.

At this same time he met a German missionary, Hanna Lechler, who Tshenu says today is "one of the living angels on earth." Hanna Lechler lived with the people, ate with them, had her home with them. According to Tshenu, this missionary lived a life of total love and was herself loved by the people. "The first time I attended her service, I won a Bible-verse competition," recalls Tshenu. He was rewarded with some sweets. "Then she said there is a God who loves you, who has created you, and has given you something sweeter than what I have given you now—he gave you his Son, Jesus Christ, who died for you." This God, who sacrificed his only Son for all humankind, Farisani found irresistible. He determined to become a pastor and preach the love that this German lady had taught him.

At secondary school, Farisani's social and political awareness was sharpened. He became a member of the Venda Students Association and at the same time taught Sunday school and was vice-chairman of the student Christian movement. The world of apartheid provided additional education. He worked for a while for a white pastor of a full-gospel church, who later beat him and kicked him out. When Farisani reported this to the police, they too beat him severely. But the love Gospel taught to him by Hanna stayed with him. He read the Bible from cover to cover and "for the first time, I was able to assess what the white people were doing to me, in the light of the Scriptures."

As a theology student in Natal from 1970 to 1972, Farisani was a member of the South African Students Organization and came into contact with Steve Biko and the Black Consciousness Movement. He would eventually rise to be the head of the Black People's Convention from 1973 to 1975, touring the country and seeing for himself the poverty of Africans throughout the republic. Always first in his class, he was expelled by the white rector of the theological school when he criticized the low wages and lack of respect given the black laborers and lecturers on campus.

Returning home, Farisani was called before the church council to explain his behavior. Farisani put his case, based on the Scriptures, and at the end of one and one half hours, the bishop accepted his argument. He finished his degree by correspondence and was given one congregation. Always a believer in strong evangelism, by the end of one year he had seen two more congregations started and seventy-seven new converts baptized. "The bishop," recalls Farisani, "was quite happy."

But the South African authorities were not as pleased. A gospel that proclaimed a God of love, justice, and equality was not the kind of gospel that produced compliant blacks. Apartheid was moving ahead, and the separation of millions of blacks from their South African citizenship into that of the created homelands was the order of the day. Early in 1977 Farisani was detained for the first time. By 1979, Venda, Farisani's home, was proclaimed an "independent" state with 750 thousand people assigned to live in its three impoverished segments. Most of its male adults had to work under contract hundreds of miles away in "white" South Africa. Venda is not recognized as independent outside South Africa.

This barren homeland is heavily dependent on support from South Africa, which provides ninety percent of its annual budget. Farisani explains that the white South Africans do not have to manipulate their chosen leaders for Venda from Pretoria, for "they are physically there in the hundreds, living in a protected white compound. Even the police interrogation chambers are in a white area."

With white South Africa's policy of divide and rule, and the large salaries given to blacks who work for it in the homeland administration and police, the threat of Dean Farisani's preaching could not be tolerated. It is this story, this witness from black South Africa, that you will now share.

Dean Farisani has no wish to be singled out, however. "I'm just one of thousands who have gone through this experience in South Africa. . . . Nor am I aware from the Biblical point of view of the prophets having it easy. It is unrealistic to expect an easy life. Jesus did not have it easy, so why should his followers?"

FIRST TIME IN
THE BOWELS OF

HELL

Heavy rains had been pouring the whole week, perhaps longer.

It was autumn in South Africa, and in good years like this one the rains continue past the summer months into February, or even March. By Sunday the thirteenth of March my Peugeot 404 wallowed through the mud on my way to preach at Ha-Mutsha, some seventeen kilometers from my home, Beuster Church Center. Beuster is the headquarters of the Devhula circuit of the Evangelical Lutheran Church in Southern Africa, Northern Diocese. This was very dangerous driving. In fact many local people call it sliding, others call it gliding, while still others call it slicing. This is by no means an adequate description of the muddy conditions that prevail, but it highlights the dangers involved for those Beuster inhabitants who dare to drive during this time. Still, after all, who cares? The people are used to it. Perhaps some even prefer it this way. Naturally, the government has only enough money for the macadamization of the streets in white towns, those roads that traverse white farms, and all the national roads. Surely no monies exist anywhere now or in the foreseeable future for the three-kilometer stretch between the hundred-year-old Beuster Church Center and the national road (long tarred) that leads to many a white man's natural dreamland—the Kruger National Park. Beuster, which is similar to many other mission centers in this part of South Africa, is the oldest springboard of the Berlin Mission Society. However, to this day no gratitude has been shown toward these centers for advancing the gospel, medical care, and education. Perhaps even God has turned a deaf ear to their plight after their many years of faithful service.

The medium-sized church always seemed to burst at its seams. On that day, young and old, men and women were in the church to listen to God's Word. Their dean, now aged twenty-nine, was with them. He preached on Matt. 20:20–28. Almost cracking the corners of his mouth, his chest expanding and contracting rhythmically, most probably responding to the inspiration of the Holy Spirit and the congregation's undivided attention, he exploded, "Mrs. Zebedee loved power. Indirectly for her own gratification and directly for her sons. Her two unfortunate sons fell into temptation. They became power drunk, power hungry. Power for the family. Yes, 'Zebedee Power.' Z.P.! Z.P.! Z.P.! at all costs. By hook or by crook, the Zebedees would seek power. They sought the authority to rule, not the privilege to serve."

About twenty minutes after the service, when many parishioners were helping themselves to a rich dinner provided by the parent of a child who had been baptized that day, the faithful servants of the "all powerful" arrived. They demanded to see the dean, who at this time was enjoying an avalanche of jokes with his boisterous congregants around a table that would make every normal pastor's heart beat with hungry excitement.

The dean, a youthful man, perhaps a little overweight for a man of just over five and a half feet, excused himself from the joyous company. Something told him that this was no friendly visitation. He walked out into the unflinching stare of the all-powerful security police. "No questions, no discussions, no delays. Get into your car and drive straight to your house. We are behind you. We shall drive behind you. Some of us are already waiting for us—for you—at Beuster Church Center. Quick! Move!"

The dean looked back at his congregation. Flabbergasted, almost numb all over, he suddenly felt very alone.

I expected God to intervene. After all, was I not preaching the truth? Was it not God who called me into ministry to preach the Word, the Word of love, justice, and equality in apartheid South Africa? I looked all around me, and finally straight into the overcast sky, but God seemed to have retired behind those unthinking black clouds. Was God perhaps on holiday?

As I drove away, the police following, the faithful church members looked on helpless. Even the three strong men who sat behind me in the church, in a spiritually supportive role, were now looking at the ground; perhaps they were appealing to the gods of Africa, who are reputed to dwell among the people and not in heaven behind the unreachable clouds.

At Ramasaga I stopped. The police also stopped. I got out of my car. They got out too. I posted a few letters in the post office box, expecting a cold bullet in the back of the head any moment—or at least a stern word. None came. Why did they not ask me what I was posting, and to whom? Would they return to open the post office box? Who could stop them?

I almost ran back to my car. In my mind I was already dodging any missiles that might come my way, verbal or otherwise. None came. A very disturbing feeling started to whirl inside me. Their ice-cold looks, their stern silence, their vengeful patience, their very presence made God's absence almost tangible. I slid into the driver's seat, and as I slammed the door, one of them shouted, "Part of your overcoat is caught in the door." I turned, surprised, and looked at the horizontal line on his face. This one had never said anything before, and I was beginning to doubt whether he even had a mouth.

The three-kilometer stretch from Ramasaga to Beuster was unpassable because of the rains and the mud; the shortest route home was out of the question. We had to snake fifteen kilometers around Sibasa instead. I waved to almost everyone I saw along the road. Some I knew, others I did not. Some returned the gesture, others did not. Was I saying goodbye to the people I so loved, or was I appealing for moral support? Was mine an aimless gesture emanating from deep frustration and fear, or did I do it to show the police that I was not afraid and had all the support in the world?

As I negotiated the dangerous curves at Tshiwamisevhe ("the place where arrows land") I shouted to everyone I saw along the road, "I am under police escort. Tell others that the dean is in the hands of the police!" Many of these people I did not know. But most of them knew me. Some would have known my car. Those who knew neither my car nor my person could at least tell others, "I saw the dean under police escort." This was very necessary, indeed vital, for in the hands of the all-powerful police, one is never able to guess what might come next. It was a comforting feeling to know that people were aware I was in police custody. Otherwise anything could happen. Some pedestrians waved back to indicate they understood the message, others just looked on in astonishment and did not return the gesture, perhaps because they did not understand. Or did they fear to invite the wrath of the all-powerful upon themselves by association?

At Ngovhela another security police car stood vigil, blockading the road to Nzhelele. Perhaps they were afraid that I might be tempted to make a daredevil escape. When I turned left, toward Beuster, the cars followed, like an obedient flock behind a good shepherd. Sliding down the muddy road was a dangerous game for me, but not for them. They were danger itself.

At Beuster a police Land Rover was neatly parked under my garage—a beautiful, large evergreen tree that is reputed to have been fully grown when Karl Beuster, the first missionary from the Berlin Mission Society, arrived in 1872. The powerful were there, in my God-given garage. I, the powerless, was forced to park my car outside. At that moment I even felt as if I was parking outside God's grace, outside God's protection. Before I came out, the other two cars had already parked my car in. Several police escorted me to the house, guns at the ready and revolvers peeping at me from hip holsters. Two police remained with my car and searched it. As we entered my house, two more police stayed outside. They and the others who searched my car started to comb the area around my house. When these things happen, even if one is innocent an indescribable fear sets in. Although I personally knew that I had nothing to hide, the behavior and attitude of the master's faithful, the ready guns, and the peeping, frowning revolvers troubled me like a guilty conscience. Perhaps, after all, I had hidden something dangerous. Was I sure that I was innocent? If I was innocent, why the creeping fear that kept growing? If I was indeed harmless, why were the police, three highly ranked whites and several blacks, so well armed and equipped for this mission?

We went into the lounge. There were at least six of them and myself. Their eyes seemed to pierce through the whole house, through the walls, through the furniture, through the pots, through the stoves, through the books, through the crucifixes on the wall, and surely through my heart. One got an impression, a very uncomfortable feeling, that they could even see the bowels of the earth. No wonder my two cousins disappeared into the kitchen immediately when they realized what was happening. When the powerful appear, the powerless disappear.

The no-entrance sign on my office door attracted the suspicious eye of one I will call Colonel White, and he issued the first command, pointing to the office door, "First, open here." For a moment I had gathered enough courage to use one of the few rights left to the black person (perhaps by an oversight on the part of the all-powerful parliament in Cape Town), the right to ask, "But you have not even shown me your search warrants; how do I know . . . ?" Even to question, I discovered to my dismay, was not a right but a privilege, a white-given privilege. "You are surely not pretending not to know us and our powers? You are wasting your time, not ours. I shall not repeat my first command, unless you want to make the atmosphere unpleasant for yourself . . . very unpleasant!" Colonel White meant business. Sergeant White's eyes were flashing threateningly. At a moment's notice, lightning would strike. Constable White was flexing his muscles, almost oblivious to his surroundings. Now the captain, a black man, was hiding behind his opaque spectacles, unseeing, unfeeling, unthinking, nonexisting. His conscience had probably long been buried by years of faithful service. The black sergeant, Anthill, as I think of him, stood there, surrounded by several smaller dark anthills, which to all intents and purposes had no living ants in them. The reason for their presence? Just to be there, like the huge anthills in Africa. They were ready for service, at the beck and call of the white colonel, sergeant, and captain.

I almost refused to open the office door, but a voice whispered within me, "But what are you hiding, Tshenu? Your sermons against injustice, discrimination, and oppression? Your uncompromising attacks against apartheid, the white man's religion? Are you not just as innocent this afternoon as you were this morning?" I fumbled among the many house keys and church-center keys for the office key. Up came key 122, and I handed it over to Colonel White. He would have to do his dirty job himself. "By God you shall open it yourself. It is your communist office, not mine." At this juncture the white sergeant added, coolly but forcefully, "More than that, Colonel, he shall not only open his communist den, he shall open his big Christian mouth, yes, his whole life to us."

"Or we shall open him up," thundered a well-trained voice through the crack on the face; and the sergeant, with his lackeys, nodded the nod of readiness to serve wherever, whenever, and in whatever manner their energies would be required. They moved around me and stamped the floor impatiently, wondering why Colonel White was so long in giving the necessary instruction, at which they would jump to prove their dedication and devotion to their master's cause, and loyalty to his structures and the philosophy that stood behind them.

"You yourselves shall open it," I said. "I am tired, exhausted after the church service. *I* have no need to go into the office. You have a need. That is your work, your job, your call. It is your mission, not mine. I am not opening; God forbid that I shall participate in the raid of a church office! Can't you read the no-entrance sign on the door? Inside are church records, posters, and congregants' personal letters, and other relevant material to which no person except authorized church officials has access. You are encroachers. This notice is meant for people like you. You have no right to meddle with church records. It is wrong, immoral, inhumane. This is terrorism in its worst form!"

At the word "terrorism" they all blushed, including the black underlings. A moment of dead silence followed. Dangerous silence. What would break this silent ice block? A punch? A kick? A bullet? The colonel laughed scornfully and said, "We shall do as he says. After all is this not the great Dean Farisani, the liberator of the oppressed? We are small, unimportant system men, and you are confused little Bantus. We shall obey the dean's orders. But let him be assured, his reign shall soon come to an end. There comes a time when even kings dance to the tune of little men like ourselves. I shall personally do as the man of God says, but he will surely discover this evening, perhaps a little later, that I did not obey him from a position of weakness. On the contrary, I am just giving a fat dog a long rope with which to hang itself."

They opened the door, and the black sergeant moved and pushed me in first. "Move into your den, commie!" I almost flew through the air in response to that push, and inside a voice said softly, "Even an elephant would shake at the slightest touch of the sergeant." Most probably his size, power, and looks were the only considerations that earned him this job. How he manages not to frighten himself remains a mystery, perhaps even to his employers. Perhaps it is the case that all things work for good not only to them that love the Lord (Rom. 8:31) but also to them that love the devil. This man, if one may call him a man, is ugly both outside and inside. He seems quite popular with his colleagues, particularly the whites, perhaps because they think his ugliness serves to exaggerate their handsomeness. My generous guess would be that he is no frequent visitor before the mirror. Once in five years would be a safe estimation.

These people have time. The whites particularly. As for the captain, the sergeant, and the other black lackeys, one wonders whether they even have the sense of time. They slowly went through my books, sermons, letters—everything that they came across. Piece by piece they handed over to the white officers every document that had something to say about the government or politics, whether for or against. Books, sermons, letters, documents, poems, speeches, university assignments were piled together as booty, confiscated simply because they contained so much as one word or phrase about the government. Some of my theological books fell into captivity simply because they discussed the kings of Israel or that part of the Lord's Prayer "Thy kingdom come!" At one stage, the sergeant came across my Greek, Latin, and Hebrew books and shouted to his colleagues at the top of his voice, with the excitement of one who had just discovered the headquarters of a terrorist gang: "Hey! Hey! Baas! Baas! Baas! Here, look. One, two, twenty. Oh! Colonel. Some more. Everywhere. I'm shocked. Ja, he is a terrorist. Look, the writing of Russia. The letters of Cuba, Mozambique, Tanzania, Tanganyika, Moscow, America, many communist. Damned. Let me handcuff him."

"Can you please read this communism to us, Dean," said the colonel, with the assurance of a conqueror.

"Willingly, sir: Bereshit barah Elohim et hashamayim veethaaretz."

"Next," the colonel commanded.

"Also willingly, sir: Ego eimi he hodos kai he aletheia kai he zoe."

"Now shall you willingly tell us what this terrorism and communism mean? Or shall you wait until you shall have to tell us under unpl . . . ?

"Now, willingly, Colonel." By now I was getting used to the idea that he liked his rank and title. "The first is Hebrew, classical Hebrew: In the beginning God created the heavens and the earth."

"And the second rubbish?" inquired the colonel.

"It's nothing sinister and evil, sir—I mean, Colonel. It is Greek, Hellenistic Greek: I am the way, the truth, and the life."

"Colonel, Colonel! My Baas! Baas! In this house, in this office, his communism and terrorism mean Hebrew class and Leninistic Greek. They all start like this. They think they are clever. We shall see to it that tonight . . . or now, if you want. These documents should mean what they mean and not what he wants them to mean. Devils, terrorists, communists." After this star performance, the captain retreated behind his spectacles.

As the hunt for dangerous documents went on, I took my Bible and started to read: "Cry aloud, spare not, lift up thy voice like a trumpet, and shew my people their transgression, and the house of Jacob their sins. . . . Is not this the fast that I have chosen? to loose the bands of wickedness, to undo the heavy burdens, and to let the oppressed go free, and that ye break every yoke? Is it not to deal thy bread to the hungry, and that thou bring the poor that are cast out to thy house? when thou seest the naked, that thou cover him? . . ." I had hardly gone through half this fifty-eighth chapter of Isaiah when the Afrikaner sergeant cast a menacing glance at me, then at the page, and after reading the first few verses he exploded, "This is the hell that we shall not stand. Always reading the wrong verses of the Bible. Stop this kak [Afrikaans for human excrement]. After all, you don't even understand the Bible. No Lutheran does. All Communists, Catholics, Lutherans, Anglicans, Methodists, English press! The Christian Institute, Black People's Convention [BPC], the South African Students Organisation [SASO], the South African Council of Churches, the World Council of Churches. Your Lutheran World Federation! All ugly organizations promoting murder and rape of children and women under the cloak of human rights—

wolves in sheep's clothing. The United Nations. Double standards. This government, my government, comes from God. Why don't you read Romans 30? [In fact he meant Romans 13.] Only one church—and I am very proud that I belong to it—preaches the true gospel in South Africa. Give this damn Bible to me!"

I watched, empty-handed and in a pensive mood, as my Bible was thrown on the floor. "God, forgive them for they know not what they do," I thought. "But do they honestly *not* know what they are doing? Should they not be punished a little to bring them to their senses? Should the devil's kingdom come into my house, the devil's will be done in the church office as in hell? And for how long?"

They searched the supply room. All the bedrooms, wardrobes. Under the carpets. Mattresses were turned inside out. Pillows too. Nothing escaped their eyes; even underwear got the touch of their roughened, detecting fingers. Socks, stockings inside out. The pantry. All the food was scattered all over the kitchen. Pots on the stove, lids lifted. A piercing look into the oven, then two loaves were taken out and opened. One should never leave a stone unturned! Communists are dangerously clever. Two, perhaps five, minutes' check of the refrigerator satisfied the microscopic eyes of Sergeant White that nothing leftist was hidden there.

From the deanery we moved to the rooms of the church center. A haphazard search was conducted. When no keys for the small church-center library were available (probably the caretaker had taken them home), one lackey suggested that the library door be forced open. Colonel White satisfied himself, however, with a piercing, searching look through the window opposite the bookshelves. When I asked to be permitted to respond to the call of nature, I was escorted by two lackeys to the toilet and I had to perform before a watchful and unloving audience. After searching the church-center premises for a while, Colonel White asked the black sergeant, "By the way have you already informed the dean that he shall be our guest today?"

"Not yet, Colonel. Let I tell now him in his mother tongue: Now we are going. You shall not sleep in your bed tonight. Come on! Go!"

I picked up my Revised Standard Version Bible and walked to their cars. The lackeys carried their masters' spoils and put them in the boot of Captain Black's car: letters, sermons, speeches, books, "Hebrew class" and "Leninistic Greek," and whatever was of interest to them. I was driven away in a police convoy, seated alone on the back seat of Captain Black's car. I waved with my Bible to my cousins, to all who had come to watch the circus, and to God. Goodbye Beuster Church Center!

Goodbye Devhula circuit! Goodbye congregations! Goodbye normal life. Goodbye peace! Goodbye health and . . . life!

At Sibasa, in offices conveniently hidden from the public eye, the booty from my office was transferred to Colonel White's car, and I, the prisoner of war, was also transferred to his car, where I occupied the back seat—unhandcuffed, un-legironed, unlocked. In front sat the white sergeant, behind the driver's wheel Colonel White himself.

"Goodbye, Constable. Well done, darkie, and you ugly ones there. It was a beautiful job well done!" At this Constable White saluted, and all the lackeys, one, two, four, six of them, jumped to do the same in response to Colonel White's final words. As the car swerved around the building, the black lackeys disappeared from view and only Constable White's hand was partially visible, albeit for a moment, as he tried to outwave his "ugly colleagues."

We went fast. The taxi was a Chrysler-built Valiant Regal. It was a new, expensive model, with many gadgets. It even had built-in tape recorders. The ride was very comfortable, even to the uncomfortable mind. Sibasa disappeared behind the horizon, along with the Beuster Church Center and the conspicuous deanery. Tshakhuma followed. Levubu was next. At Ratombo Sawmills, the sergeant looked back for the first time, "Are you comfortable, Dean?"

"Very," I replied.

"Are you healthy?"

I hesitated, since I could not understand the necessity of the second question. Then the sergeant, as if to answer himself, came in just when I was about to answer, "Not very," and said, "Don't worry. Healthy or not healthy, we shall do our job. After all, unhealthy people should know better how to look after themselves, what to say, and what to preach."

"Perhaps," Colonel White chipped in, "they should know that Romans 13 is better than Isaiah 58, that we live in New Testament times, not Old Testament times. But," he sighed, "perhaps we have already said too much prematurely. The dean will need a peaceful sleep before we undertake the next long lap of our trip. We can only hope that by now he realizes that he is not in the pulpit or in his office. This is our sphere of influence."

In Louis Trichardt the white officers handed me over to two black lackeys and gave instructions about food and other matters only under- stood among themselves. The lackeys then led me into a small room with blinds, and locked the door behind us. They gave me a rugged bench to sit on (probably made in a hurry during the Anglo-Boer war of 1899– 1902) while they sat on two comfortable chairs. They just sat there . . .

and sat . . . and sat. They looked at me all the time, but did they actually see me? I looked around the room. At the right corner lay a wooden knob-kerrie (club) next to which were heavy iron weights such as amateur weight lifters use in the countryside. "What are they for?" I asked myself. Before I could discover the answer, which in any case would never come, I saw on the table next to the window a square cardboard box, torn at one edge, through which shining nails peeped at me. Probably—I could not make sure at this distance—the nails were affixed to a plank, for purposes only known to the two lackeys who sat lifeless before me. Many thoughts—terrible thoughts—flashed through my increasingly unsettled mind: Surely they don't mean . . . they cannot do it . . . they would not go that low . . . at least not with a D . . . Did I want to say a Dean? An owl outside greeted his friend on a tree across the street, and the dead men in the blind-drawn room came to life.

"What do you need to eat, Dean?" asked a sergeant. He was too light in complexion for an African in this part of the world.

"I am not hungry, Const . . . Serge . . . Captain." I searched for the right title. Who knows, knowing their titles might in the long run save one from the peeping nails!

"Are you sure you will not want something to eat? The night shall be long, and things may . . . " I did not wait to hear the last part of his statement.

"Anything, Captain, I'll eat anything."

"I am not a captain in the first place. But you need not worry, not now. I will get you something to nibble on. The other constable will look after you. Do not try, do not even *think* something stupid. You are a clever man. You can make things easy or difficult for yourself. The choice is yours." The sergeant (I don't care, I named him) then turned to his constable with an air of contemptuous authority and issued his first command: "If the Dean does something stupid, do not hesitate to . . . "

I could hear him snoring. His eyes were closed, his mouth wide open. A large green fly walked up and down the valley and hills of the constable's triangular face. One small misstep and that fly would land deep in the bottomless throat. "Should one open the door stealthily and disappear into nowhere?" I wondered. "Perhaps push this lump of flesh on the innocent chair upside down, take his revolver, his handcuffs, and . . . "

"What are you thinking, Dean? Is it possible . . . ?"

"Nothing, Constable," I interrupted apologetically. "Only that I am feeling . . . "

"You'd better not feel anything, not think anything, not plan anything, not hope anything. You'd better not see anything, either. This is not the place for it. Here people hear what we say and do what they are told." With this illuminative lesson at an end, the constable again fell into a deep sleep, and this time his snores almost shook his endless frame apart.

"How does he dare . . . ?" I reached my wit's end and plunged into a silent prayer: "Why all this, God? Why me, Lord? Why grant so much power to this cruel creature before me? The evil man prospers in his evil ways while . . . Amen." I was stopped in my tracks, perhaps by the latent fear that the "prophet" before me would again read my mind but probably because an unexpected scream came either from the street nearby or the next room.

The supper was a decent one: one hamburger, one meat pie, two boiled eggs, and a pint of fresh milk. After this I was escorted to the toilet outside the building. "Please discharge all the water and the food you have in your body. We will not afford to go up and down the whole night because the dean wants to perform rites in the toilet. Sorry for the words. But they are true. Aren't they?"

That night I slept on a canvas folding bed, in my clothes. I had only my clothes: one pair of shoes and socks, one pair of trousers and underpants, one shirt and vest, one jacket, and one T-shirt. I was just an orderless lump of flesh between two powerful, dedicated, and trusted servants of the state. My prayer was short and simple. This was no time for luxuriant theological phrases. After all, only God would be listening, and no congregants would be present to admire my "proper" English. I prayed, in my mother tongue, Mphe khofhe Baba. Ivha Mulisa wanga ("Give me sleep, my Father. Be my shepherd").

The Trip to Nowhere

"Up . . . up . . . up . . . up . . . get up!" I emerged from my peaceful sleep and wondered who this was who awoke me so violently. I struggled to reconstruct the environment and the circumstances. Fortunately, a helping voice came to rescue my wandering mind. "This is not Beuster, man! You are not a dean here. Terrorist, we are not your congregation! You should get used to getting up at midnight. All communists are!" I looked at my trusted Seiko watch. Two in the morning! Like an obedient sheep, I followed Colonel White and his snow-white colleague, while the faithful black lackeys tailed me. We marched to the Valiant Regal, and to the seat of honor. I was not handcuffed, not leg-ironed, but free. To the uninitiated eye, I might have been a willing passenger, perhaps co-worker, . . . no, probably a garden boy with many years of faithful service.

A countdown on my freedom, my human dignity, had begun. Louis Trichardt, Bandelierkop, Botlokwa. Destination: Pietersburg? No, we passed the junction to Zebediela, then Potgietersrust.

"Do you know where we are taking you, Dean?" asked Colonel White politely.

"No sir, I do not. But does that matter? After all, wherever you take me, there will my God be." But was I really sure that God would be there? If my God was not there when they trampled upon my rights by detaining me on Sunday, the holy day, the day before, could I still rely on God?

"We shall lock you up in Pietermaritzburg, one thousand kilometers from your home," retorted Sergeant White, victoriously. So it was not to be Compol Building, a torture center in Pretoria, not John Vorster Square. Pietermaritzburg—what happens there? Only God knows . . . if God really cares to know! We snaked down the road, down, down, down, into Natal, mostly in uncomfortable silence. Pietermaritzburg was not unfamiliar to me, but now I wondered whether I really knew it. In which dark corner of this city would I eventually land?

Somewhere along the way we stopped. It was in a small town, a nameless country town. If it had a name, I did not care to know. We walked together to a small restaurant, and as we walked out we each carried a hamburger, a meat pie, Russian and Vienna sausages, and a liter of fresh milk. I did not eat. I walked to a dirty, nonwhite toilet around the building. Nobody asked me where I was going, nobody even cared to look at me. I performed quickly, and we drove on as if nothing had happened. Down-up-down, down, down-up, down. A hundred kilometers per hour! A hundred twenty! A hundred forty! A hundred . . . ! "Truly," I said inwardly, "these people can do what they like. The ninety-kilometer speed limit is not meant for them. They are surely above the law."

"Dean," Colonel White glanced at me as we negotiated one of the many dangerous mountain curves, "how long will it take to persuade you to stop all your childish ideas?"

"Which ideas, Colonel?" I asked.

"Don't you realize you are playing with fire?" He went on, as if my question had not been directed at him, "You are an intelligent young man. South Africa—I mean Venda—would make you a very important person if only you could see things properly, if only you could see the light."

"But, Colonel, how can one see light in apartheid, equality in discrimination, love in hatred, trust in suspicion, life in death, and God in the devil? How can one see proper things in an improper system? Colonel, I am afraid I cannot agree with you; if at least I have to be honest with myself."

Dead silence. The Valiant nearly failed to take the next curve. Now the sergeant was literally expanding and contracting with anger before my eyes, seething with uncontrollable fury. He exploded, "And what about the four young boys that you sent to Botswana for terrorist training last year?"

"For terrorist training, Colonel, I mean, Sergeant? Did I hear you properly?"

He shook, and turned red, very red. "Colonel! Colonel, I cannot stand this nonsense any longer. If you can not control this bloody [expletive deleted] dean of yours I am afraid I may . . . !"

The Colonel turned to me with a sinister grin. Then the inside of the car thundered as he unleashed his laughter from the darkest corners of his being: "Leave your fury to the younger boys, Sergeant. It is difficult for the dean to know anything in this dirty uncomfortable car. When he is in his hotel room this afternoon, he will remember things he has never known. They all start out like this, but don't they always end up the right way? At least that should be your experience in your twenty years of service, Sergeant."

We turned right, then left, then north, then south, then north again, north-west, west-west, south-north, right, left, right—oh, I lost direction!

"Here Colonel, to your right. We are there." It was an innocent-looking building. We walked in. They walked into an office; I remained in the hallway. I could hear whispers but could not follow what they said. "It does not matter; God hears what they are saying. These stupid whispers are like trumpet sounds in his ears. God is tape-recording these sinister whispers; one day they will be broadcast over Radio Revelation," I whispered to myself.

They brought me some food. I left it alone. A handsome young man, one of the security police, appeared from nowhere. "Why don't you eat your food, Dean, such good food!"

"Sir," I said, "I told your colonel already on the way that the fourteenth of every month is a special day set aside for prayer, not for feasting. If it is allowed, I shall eat this food tomorrow."

As we drove to the prison, the young man's eyes turned red, uncompromisingly threatening, "Do you know the SACC [South African Council of Churches]? The CI [Christian Institute]? The BPC? SASO?

The PAC [Pan African Congress] and ANC [African National Congress]?" Before I could answer, he added, "Will you tell the truth?"

"Yes, I shall tell the truth." At this answer I got a feeling of being turned into a machine, a traffic light. "Will you tell your truth?" There I was: I had just turned green at his command, now I had again to turn amber at his whim. A feeling of complete helplessness enveloped my whole being as I managed, like a machine without enough current, to slip the reply through my uncooperative teeth: "The truth."

He smiled, then burst into a deafening laugh and asked, "Since when do these communist churches tell the truth? Shall I not rather rely on the devil than on these people? If this one tells the truth, he will be the first outside our church—a real breakthrough. Perhaps water can still turn into wine. Is it not my personal experience that in South Africa we do not find gold on the surface anymore? We have to dig deep, very deep. Any way! Any way at all!"

When we reached the prison entrance, he was still shaking his head in learned disbelief. Deep down I wondered, "Since when is truth a welcome species in South Africa? Is a swine asking for pearls?"

The End of the World

At Pietermaritzburg prison, my young security police escort pressed the prison-gate button. (Falsesnow is the name I gave to this handsome young man, the "lover of truth.") Someone from behind the imposing iron gate peeped through a small hole. The security policeman showed his card. The door opened and my world closed. A second gate opened, and a third. We went into a small room, perhaps a charge office. Many other black men were present, naked, in a row. I joined the new world of the naked. My personal items—belt, watch, and about thirteen rand—were taken into "safety." After satisfying themselves that my clothes were nothing more than clothes, the two local lackeys allowed me to dress, but not until they had felt into my shoes and socks, and touched my body all over—very professionally.

A woman sat behind the counter and took my personal details: name, address, age, profession, etc. Then, looking at me with the utmost contempt she said, "What have you done?"

"Nothing, madam." I clenched my teeth and held my breath.

"Madam is your black kaffir ass [kaffirgat]. Sergeant, take this baboon from me. I . . . I . . . ." Evil words battled for the way and blocked her throat.

"To him there's no missis and no Baas," said the sergeant. "He calls us sir and now he calls you madam. Tonight he shall know the difference.

Write Section Six of 1967 [a no-trial detention act]. He is a terrorist. All of them are terrorists, the whole church and their organizations . . . devils, satans, communists."

I got my card. On it were my number and date of admission. And my crime: terrorism. The door closed behind me, then another door. At the entrance of a large building I got a cell number. It was not on the ground floor, not on the floor above. One, two, three gates closed behind me. Then I moved into my cell—my house, my circuit, my country, my world. "That is your hotel room," said my escort. "Communism flourishes in mansions of this nature. Preach your sermons. Deliver your speeches. Drive your Peugeot. Be the dean. The sky is the limit." The young white policeman smiled at the guard, who returned the smile approvingly. That was the last I saw of him. Then bang! Bang! Solitary confinement. In my cell behind a door, an iron-grille door, and another door. I tried to count how many doors and gates I would have to conquer if I were forced to seek my own freedom: one, three, five . . . oh, it was better not to know. I looked at my Bible, and the *Sunday Times* I bought in the nameless town. "Why did I take these innocent items into prison, into this lonely cell one thousand kilometers from home? Perhaps I should apologize to the newspaper and the food. Not to the Bible. It is responsible for my detention. The Word of God has landed me in trouble. God is responsible. The Bible must suffer with me . . . perhaps this newspaper too. Its critical approach to apartheid has infected me. This food too . . . we are fighting for equality to get enough food for every black mouth. We all deserve to be here: you, Bible; you, *Sunday Times*; you, food. Do you hear me, terrorists? Or are you communists? Subversive elements."

One mat and one blanket lay rolled at one corner. At another was a toilet bucket. A strong smell came from the direction of the blanket. On closer investigation it became clear that the greasy bedding had seen many sleepless nights. The smell of the disinfectant in the bucket did not make matters any easier. The smell was very sickly and piercing. I started to pace the cell: one, two, three, three and a half. Now the distance from the door to the back wall: one, two, three, four. No, I had hardly stretched my legs too. One, two, three, yes, three and a half.

"Hope it will grow larger at night," came a voice in Afrikaans out of nowhere. Caught in my tracks, I sat down, and felt very stupid. Perhaps I even looked very stupid, like a green mamba in a glass cage watched by school children singing a mock victory chorus: "Mamba, mamba, now we have you, now we see you, now we know you. We may not tame you, but we can keep you!"

The door opened, and before me stood a tall black phantomlike figure: "Woza [come on], exercise." I followed. At least my legs carried me behind this citizen of the kingdom of the dead. Inside, the self protested. My human dignity rebelled. From the remotest corner of my person a voice rang: "Now they have you. They call the tune; you dance. Even ghosts shall lead you in and out." As I followed, I got a very uncomfortable feeling of being turned into a machine.

Once outside, I looked at the gathering clouds above my head with mixed feelings of gratitude and unclarified fear. Is it not wonderful to be outside the cell? But for how long?

Dlala mfowethu, ngithi dlala . . . isikathi siyakushiya baba ("Play my brother, play. . . you are wasting your exercise time"). He was very impatient, this angel from the dead.

"What shall I play?" I asked.

Dlala mfowethu ngithi dlala, he repeated.

"Let me have a football, to kick by myself, or is there any. . . ?"

Ngena, phakathi ("Come inside. You don't like to play"). I followed, feeling ten times more stupid than when I went out.

Supper found me retracing the whole trip from Beuster to my present home. Soft porridge with a very dark soup sprayed on top. Honestly, it looked like human excrement topped with vomited beer. It did not even occur to me that I was expected to attend to this mess in the contorted brass dish that had seen many years of very dedicated service. My world had immediately come to an end: no company, no freedom of movement, no say about my food, no choice of accommodation. I was a creature without rights, a nonbeing. World without end. Amen.

At the Red Sea

When one dreams of water, particularly blue waters, our grandmothers regard it as a sign for good. But when one dreams of water, and wakes to find oneself in a pool, that is a problem! As I came to, a flash followed by a peal of thunder reawakened my five senses to the realities of the heavy rain outside. A cold drop landed on my nose, and as I turned round, another, even more uncompromising, exploded in my ear. Many more landed all around me. In fact, I later realized, this performance had been going on for hours. Not only were the mat and blanket drenched but the water had also awakened the latent smells in the bedding, making the air in the cell very sour.

I used the blanket to dry the floor, wringing the water into the toilet bucket. Every time I made some progress, more rain came in a counterattack. My reservoir, the bucket, was also threatening to fill up any minute. When it eventually did fill up, I gave up the struggle. It is bad enough to face the police alone, but when nature (and God) comes on their side, the struggle is as good as lost. Nevertheless, in the painful process of losing the struggle against the elements I did not lose my will to survive. I walked from corner to corner. Every time the water volume increased in one corner, I would move to another, and then to the next, and back to the first. It was very cold. Morning seemed milleniums away. Then there was light in the cell, light from outside. An inquisitive eye looked through a glass hole in the door, the size of a policeman's eye but a little bigger and more spherical. I waved and shouted, but the ghost had long disappeared, leaving no footprints and no hope. In the distance, now in the company of the dead, he exploded into mock laughter, and another voice said, Laat hy dans ("Let him dance"). How much I wished I could see the face of this man.

My mind turned to God, a power and source beyond myself. All my efforts had failed. I desperately needed a trusted ally. The fight within me was not dead. I only needed a ground, a height from which to survey, a platform from which to continue my struggle. But could I really see? Was there really any spring in my bones? "God," I said, "you parted the waters of the Red Sea in the process of liberating your oppressed children from the cruel hand of the almighty Pharaoh. It should be a small matter for you to remove these few liters so that I, your pastor, may sleep on dry land." There was no reaction, no miracle, no hope, no future, no liberation for oppressed prisoners. Perhaps there was no God! "God, if you don't want to remove this pool (or can't you?), please turn me into a frog so that I may be at home and sing songs of praise on the bank." At that moment I accepted my new environment—all conditions inclusive. I felt like a frog, very wet all over, my clothes as well. I began to jump in circles in the water, hop, hop, hop! Then I sang in my froglike voice,

> Defeat the cell,
> Conquer the smelling bedding,
> Consume the messy food,
> Trample the water into pieces,
> Dry South Africa of apartheid,
> Be prisoner, be drenched, be frog,
> Above all, make sure you will be free—one day!

Even frogs get tired, but they can be clever in the art of survival. God sees to that. I poured the water out of the bucket (thank God I had not used it yet) and placed it next to the door, where the floor was apparently slightly higher. I turned it upside down and sat.

DAY
ONE

"Skik, skik, skik, skik, skik, skik!" It was already morning, to be sure, very early. "Skik" in prison language, I later discovered, means "toilet bucket." The ghost repeatedly pointed to it, and I put it outside the cell, in the narrow passage flanked by cells on both sides. A few minutes later the ghost threw pieces of cloth into my cell, and a large tin. He then floated away, lifelessly. I had understood the instruction. I mopped up the water. It was not until the large tin was almost full that I could actually dry the floor.

Immediately after this, breakfast came, as pale as the ghost who brought it. Soft porridge, heavily salted, and another dish, coffee as black as a typical nonwhite. The mealiemeal must have been in waiting for a long time if the tiny, slender soft worms were anything to go by. The coffee looked like roasted wood ground into black powder for kaffir (black) terrorist consumption. The dish had already lost its original brassy color to align itself with its more powerful contents, kaffirbrew. Alone before my meal, I refused to eat. A dean cannot eat this rubbish! A member of diocesan council, of diocesan synod, of church council, and of the general assembly . . . surely, he shall never touch this slop.

I had not eaten the previous day. I had fasted regularly before but never for more than a day. The previous night I had swallowed all the food the Egyptians bought for me on the way. That morning the wet *Sunday Times* I had brought in with me was confiscated by the ghost. Only the Revised Standard Version remained. I could read it—but not eat it. I was growing hungrier by the minute. The meal before me was turning from slop to a mess of blood and guts. I broke into prayer with eyes as wide-open as the largest ocean. I could no longer afford the luxury of blind prayer. That belongs to the dean's table full of mouthwatering meals at Beuster. Here I was faced with worms and kaffirbrew. Both looked at me with cruel, discomforting eyes, arrogant as the stubborn doors behind me. "God," I said, "Yahweh, you provided the oppressed, persecuted Israelites with food in the wilderness. I cannot—I do not want to—eat these sausages before me. Remove this vinegar from before my eyes. Give me manna and heavenly meat as you did the Jews. Surely you do not expect me to wallow in this mess." Amen was another luxury I could not afford. For a minute I closed my eyes, sensing the unwillingness of providence to let manna fall in broad daylight, in full human view. I waited for the sound of dropping manna and meat, and when it came, I opened my eyes. There, before me, lay the well-known kaffirbrew, now very sticky and cold, and the worms, larger and fatter. I stood and marched to the door, and commanded in the name of the triune God, "Hardened iron grilles, stubborn doors and arrogant locks, I command you in the name of Yahweh the Father, of Jesus Christ the Son, and of the Holy Spirit, be opened and let the servant of the Lord go free and buy himself food suitable for a man of his standing!" There was no sign of movement, no sign that these bloody cruel wood and iron masses had heard. There they stood, spitting directly into the face of God and this servant, more powerful than the Almighty. Surely, when and where the police have locked, no one can unlock—not even the heavens dare do that. One thing became clear: either God favors the whites over against the blacks and is practicing holy apartheid or God has simply been overthrown from power. How else does one explain God's benevolent attitude to whites and God's negligence in the Pietermaritzburg wilderness?

I turned around, sat down, sorted the sausages from the soft porridge as far as was humanly possible, and filled my terrorist stomach. Several times my stomach wanted to set the food free, but I forced myself to keep it down. Was this not the only way to hold on to whatever life was left me? The nonsugared brew would go back untouched, at least for today.

Then three white images were ushered in. One introduced himself as a magistrate, and the other two remained unidentified. "Any complaints?" asked the magistrate. "Yes, I have. I am innocent. Why should I be kept in prison, and worst of all, in this terrible cell with smelly bedding and a bucket toilet? Drenched by rain all night . . . terrible food with worms . . . undrinkable coffee . . . no toilet paper . . . no reading books . . . I want to be free to go home to my work."

"What work do you do?" asked the magistrate, almost scornfully.

"I am a pastor, a dean of the Lutheran church, a man of God, a man of truth."

"If he were a pastor—a true pastor—he would not be here," said one of the two UTOs (unidentified torturing objects). The magistrate nodded in agreement, and instructed the ghost to look for a cell with better roofing and to provide me with dry bedding. The other complaints were ignored. They were happy to have created an image of justice and care for the detainees, and as they walked out, I could hear the chief image saying, "So he thinks he is innocent. They all start by saying so. Before long he will be telling a different story." Both UTOs nodded with approval; the ghost locked the cell doors and floated faithfully behind his gods, to the next detainee.

Lunch came, maize with worms, and vegetable soup on top. Except for the sausages, this was tastier than the soft porridge. An iron mug contained the prison brew known as *phuzamandla*, which means "energy drink." This provides energy in the body of black "donkeys" before they are put to labor. I hated the smell and the taste of it. In fact I had previously been told that this brew is used to tame the masculinity of black prisoners. I am not yet persuaded to believe these stories, but I shall not go out of my way to prove them wrong. In South Africa everything is possible, or better, nothing is impossible.

I spent the afternoon walking up and down the streets of the cell, passing the time. When the exercise period came—which was usually five minutes, and only by accident up to ten minutes—I ran in circles, hopped, stepped, and jumped, and stretched my arms in the air until I was sweating all over. After what seemed to be three minutes, the unsmiling white guard summoned me back to the cell, by the movement of his powerful arm. "May I please have a bath? I have not had any for two days."

"You either have a bath or exercise. You can not have both. Just this morning you opened your bloody [expletives] to tell the magistrate that you slept in a pool of water! What more bathing do you want? To bathe until you are white? You think we are playing here. Jy sal kak, in jou broekie! [You will . . . in your pants]." I walked straight into my open cell, and all the doors banged shut behind me. Long after the white guard had left, his words remained ringing in my head, stinging like robbed bees.

Supper brought a welcome surprise: some soft porridge, but this time with meat soup, presided over by a big piece of meat (from what animal I did not care to know). I did not even check whether the sausage was hidden in the porridge. I just swallowed and swallowed. Perhaps I was even a little grateful. When the light went off (they controlled it from outside the cell, in the passage), I had already gone through the whole primeval history of Genesis (chaps. 1—11). I prayed and slept. For one long, peaceful hour I played in the warm arms of mother sleep, until a noise, a sharp scream, a human scream of agony, shook me violently out of my sleep, as a bomb shatters a pane of glass: "Ngiafa baba, ngiafa baba [I am dying, Daddy]. Ho! Ho! Hoo! Hooooooo! Hmm! Hmmmmmmm! No! No! No! Nononononononono! Ngiafa baba! I do not know!...I do not know!...Yes! yes! yes! Yeeeees! Yeeesss! YYYYeesss!"

"We told you you would know—and now you know. Jy sal die waarheid praat [You will tell the truth]. Anders sal jy dit uikkak [Otherwise you will have to excrete it]."

I had to listen to screams like these for almost three months. It was the most terrifying period of my life. One time, the victim was my neighbor. Another time, in a cell far away only faint screams could be heard, this time to my right, next time to my left, then opposite the passage, again in the cells below. At times the screams came from outside, sometimes drowned by running car engines or the barking of police dogs. But always, in a mysterious way, the human screams would filter through all the disguises and reach my human ear, breaking my human heart. Then I would fall on my knees and cry softly, at times silently, to the Lord despite my previous disappointments with him: "Oh God, you source of justice and love, opponent of oppression and exploitation, enemy of apartheid and torture, where are you? The murderers are let loose. The wolves are plundering. Can't you hear the desperate screams, the begging for mercy, the forced confessions? Can't you hear the boasting of the godless? Where is your love? Where is your care and concern? Where is your being? Please God, let them come to torture me rather than have me listen to the screams of my brothers and sisters. Amen. No, I cannot say amen. I ask you to help them. Not tomorrow, tonight. Will you? Unless you do, you are in a way participating in their torture, and in my torment." Usually my prayer would flow on as long as the screams and groans could be heard. As they subsided, I would also sink gradually into the uncomfortable bosom of the thorny mat, cover my body up to the breast with the smelly blanket, and disappear into the dying screams of the unseen—the unprotected and the nonhumans. Then I would join the sleeping city all around me, sleeping South Africa, and the sleeping universe under the control of its sleeping God—leaving the fresh screams unheard except by the unsympathetic ear. In the morning it was almost possible to estimate the damage done by listening to the sound of the victim's footsteps, or the victim's voice when asking for toilet paper, or the victim's response to the hypocritical question "Any complaints?"

FREEDOM
WAITS

The Blank Wall

Minutes in prison are long. Every hour has three hundred and sixty minutes. Every day seventy-two hours. Every week equals a month outside. One has to find a means of remaining alive or die. There is no dawn, no sunrise, no afternoon, no evening—only night.

Every morning I prayed. My amen was often the ghost's familiar cry at the door, "Skik!" Then the sound of the keys in three locks, and the door would open. I would leap forward, pick up the bucket, usually littered on the bottom with very unfriendly contents, and place it in the passage. Then the ghost would lock the outside door without uttering a single word in the world.

A few minutes later, not everyday, the door would open again and the other bucket with dead water, covered with a creamy substance and lint from the mat and blanket, would be replaced with "fresher" water, only to be covered with the same substance before noon. Often I disliked drinking this unhealthy brew, but I liked the idea of having two buckets in my cell, one my toilet, the other my water tap. On days when I was not allowed a shower in the cubicle on the ground floor, this second bucket served as my bath water too. I would wet my hands and wipe my face, as well as the sensitive areas that tended to emit a very unpleasant odor when I missed a shower for two or three days. At times it was a whole week between showers. Of course I did not always dislike the idea of being kept away from the shower, since the water was always ice-cold, as unsympathetic and as unfeeling as the ghost. More, the white guard would always look at my nakedness with disgust, then spit on the floor

and shout, "Enough! Cover your swart gat [black ass] before I vomit."
With the nimbleness of a possessed man I would jump into my filthy
clothes, raising the smell of their dirt from the dead by the undried water
on my body.

After breakfast I studied the Bible, usually Old Testament, since New
Testament was reserved for the afternoon. I read and read, and
meditated—pondered on this and that—for hours on end. This might
have helped to "kill time," but the main thing was that I had developed
an interest in the Holy Scriptures which I had never had before. Not that
I had ever lacked interest; it had always been there. But now it was more
intense. It had broadened and deepened. It had become vibrant, active,
and alive. Measured by thermometer, it had reached the boiling point. In
the first thirteen days I had traversed the Bible from cover to cover, and
this feat was to be repeated several times in the next two months.

My cell was dirty, very dirty. For the first two or three days I did not
give a damn. What is the use, after all, of keeping a cell clean? For what
purpose? The mat and blanket are dirty and smelling. Full of human
sweat and secretions. Bugs, thorns—everything is dirty. The water is covered with a jelly of filth. My toilet was always staring at me, boasting its
unsmiling contents, frowning at the owner. Dirt everywhere. Dirty I.
Dirty cell. Dirty mouth full of unbrushed teeth growing a distasteful
layer around the gums and into the roots.

> Dirty universe
> Dirty gods
> Dirty creation
> Dirty South Africa
> Dirty laws
> Dirty police
> Shall I clean dirty teeth in a rotting mouth
> Shall I wipe a dirty face on a dirty head
> Cover a clean body in smelling clothes
> Cover my kaffirgat in filthy pants
> By my sister[1] Tshinakaho the beautiful
> By the grace of the dead gods of Africa
> I shall not sweep a dirty cell in a dirty prison
> I shall not clean a dirty prison in a dirty country
> By Mutshinya the destruction
> By the power of the blackness of my ass
> Apartheid shall I sweep away
> Security-evil-laws blow to pieces

---

[1]In my culture, we swear by our sister, to attest that something is true. My first sister is
Tshinakaho ("the beautiful") and my second sister, Mutshinya ("the destruction").

Then shall South Africa be clean as the blue sky
Clean of prisons
Clear of ghosts
Clean of torture
Clear of color
Silent night, silent night
Clean child, our clear future

I refused to clean my cell. First of all, there would be no aim in it. Or did I perhaps hope for an early release? Afternoons could be very lonely. To break the solitude, I would put the rolled blanket and mat on the toilet bucket, climb, and look through the small window facing away from the passage. Before me at a distance, a concrete jungle, cut by narrow snakelike streets, with cars the size of a loaf of bread. Occasionally, particularly on weekends, I would strain my eyes to watch a soccer match some kilometers away. I would be captivated, not because I could actually see the ball but just because I enjoyed watching the fast movements of the players, now here, now there, jumping into the air, now in a slide fall, then in a pile of human bodies near the goal, in midfield, everywhere. "Get down from there!" The ghost was looking at me through the peephole. "I shall . . . ngizobabhiza [call the whites]." In no time the ghost was back with a white policeman, the door opened, he pointed at me and left. We stood face to face, man to man, police to prisoner, free to unfree. For two solid minutes his eyes pierced through my fragile forehead, and almost through the bridge of my nose. He shook his head, and as the door closed between us, he spit one word: "Kaffir!" From that day on, I had to make doubly sure, before I took my position at the soccer "stadium," that the coast was clear. I was not always successful: I was caught on two other occasions, but on both occasions the police overlooked my crime, perhaps having realized that it was a sort of disease caused by the germ of loneliness in the unhygienic atmosphere of solitary confinement.

Monday, Tuesday, Wednesday, Thursday, Friday, Saturday, Sunday, Monday, Tuesday, Wednesday, Thursday, Friday, Monday . . . no, Saturday, Friday . . . , no Sunday. Long morning, long afternoon, long evening, long night. Terrible darkness. Screams. Heavy footsteps in the passage. A round eye through the peephole in the cell door. At times every fifteen minutes. At times hourly. At times not at all. When would they come for me? When would I join my screaming neighbors? What were they plotting against me? Would I go out alive? Or would I never go out? The present was a painful uncertainty, the future total darkness, the past an irretrievable reality.

Thursday, Friday, Saturday, and Sunday, March 27, 1977, were all days of prayer and fasting. I took no water, no coffee, no soft porridge, no maize grains. Prayer for breakfast. Prayer for lunch. Prayer for supper. Prayer at midnight. Prayer. Prayer. Prayer. "God, I plead with you, answer my prayer. I am suffering very badly in the cell. Have I committed a crime? Do I deserve this suffering? Perhaps it is sinful that I preached against apartheid. Let me know. Perhaps, after all, apartheid is your will, the Pretoria government your creation, my suffering a due portion of your wrath upon the unrighteous. I want to know. I *must* know. I have to know. It is unfair that I should suffer in ignorance. If I have to suffer, let it be with a purpose. Aimless suffering is unbearable torture. Amen. Amen. Amen."

The Lord's reply was like pepper on an open wound: "You have a car, but do you help the poor along the road? Your wardrobes are bulging with clothes, some not even your size any longer, but do you care to share with the needy? You preach morality and purity, but are you dead to sin and truly alive in Christ, even in your mind? Repent!"

It was March 26, just before the light went off at eight o'clock. I lay on my mat; my rolled blanket served as a pillow. I was totally absorbed in Psalm 121. All of a sudden there was a flash in my cell, there was a dazzling brightness that pierced even into my mind. I crossed into another world. Security policemen stood before me: "Are you Tshenuwani Farisani?"

I said, "Yes, I am."

Their leader, an ugly menacing white dragon with protruding teeth, grinned. "We have come to fetch you. Forget about the Bible. Get dressed! Quick! We're going."

As I stood up to comply, the bright light disappeared as it had come, and with it the security police. I was again alone, prostrate on my mat, my Bible on my chest, sweating heavily. The doors and the grille were securely locked as before, there were no footsteps or voices in the passage. I knelt and prayed, "Father, thank you for your revelation, for the vision. What does it mean? Amen." I collapsed onto my mat, and slid into deep sleep. Not even the sharpest screams could have penetrated my cell this night.

The Wait Is Over

It was morning . . . afternoon . . . evening . . . March 27. There were footsteps in the passage, voices, then a light in my cell. The door opened.

This was my turn. After fourteen days of waiting, blank waiting, now they were here. Before sunrise, the clean sheets would be blue with ink, and a lot of nonsense.

"Are you Tshenuwani Farisani?"

"Yes sir, I am."

"What is your profession?"

"Dean of the Evangelical Lutheran Church in Southern Africa."

"What is your profession, man? Do not waste my time, what kak is this din? Do you . . . ?"

"I preach and supervise . . . "

"You are dominie . . . a pastor . . . a kaffir dominie?"

"Yes, I preach, I am a pastor."

His colleagues watched. He grinned "Get dressed. Quick! We go!" I reached for my Bible. "Leave it!"

For a moment I hesitated, then almost involuntarily I murmured, "But I need it. I shall need it."

"Let him take it, Captain. By midnight he will have forgotten about it. It may be interesting to the Bible to watch what we can do to its dean!"

Handcuffed, I was led through the innumerable doors and gates. It was good to walk outside, good to watch the stars and the clear sky. The feeling of being free from the dulling atmosphere of the cell, my home for the previous two weeks, made me forget about what awaited me. Handcuffed to the back of the pickup, legs manacled in irons to a crossbar. The pain began to sting. I pleaded that my legs not be crossed. Captain White barked, "He knows how to handle communists. You will not teach him his job!" Indeed, the lackey did a perfect job. "If you like you can jump off the van and run to your communist brothers in Tanzania." The lackey leaped into the back of the van and sat next to me. "You have done an excellent job last night," said Captain White, "today, and also now. Come, three of us can sit in front." Then, turning to me, grinning his white, shining teeth menacingly in the dim street lighting, the captain said, "Dean, be comfortable. We apologize that the state cannot afford a canopy for this bakkie [pickup] as the money goes to combating terrorism. Keep the wind out of the bakkie with your prayers. I wish you a good trip."

We sped away from Pietermaritzburg, at perhaps 140 kilometers per hour. I froze in the ice-cold wind and wriggled as the handcuffs cut into my flesh and pain seared my twisted limbs. Contradictory desires clashed in my mind: "The sooner we reach our destination, the better. I cannot bear these pains any longer. . . . The longer it takes to reach our destination, the better. The wind is cold but fresh, the present pains nothing compared with what I may suffer once we reach our destination."

We followed the arrow to Howick police station. Handcuffed and leg-ironed, I struggled up the steps to the third floor. My legs felt numb. Three were waiting for me. "Let him sit on this chair, like a *gentleman*." I sat. Before me stood the officer in charge, this hefty tower of white muscles, eyes half closed, the large nostrils pulling in eighty-seven per-cent of the oxygen between us. I was worried more by what I could not see than by what I could see. The two bullies behind me kept stamping the floor and saying between themselves, "Let us wait and see if we shall be needed." Now it was the turn of the white giant: "Can you tell us something about amalgamation?"[2]

Astonished, I reacted, almost involuntarily: "Amalgamation! What is amalgamation?"

The officer turned round and shouted as if possessed, "Gentlemen! Come! Come, gentlemen! We shall need your services!" Punches. Kicks. Punches. Kicks. Punches. Kicks. Pushed. Pulled. Pushed. Pulled. Pushed. Pulled. Hair pulled out. Beard uprooted. Carried in the air by my hair. I was thrown on the floor, then commanded to stand. Thrown on the floor. Commanded to stand. It was a long, very long, hour. Per-haps two, perhaps three. Perhaps thirty minutes. The thunders of the blows and the thuds were punctuated by my groaning and the occasional shouts by the possessed three: "Enemy of my country! Communist! Ter-rorist! Die! Die! Die! Kill! Kill! Amalgamation! Botswana! Amalgama-tion! Botswana boys![3] Enemy of my country! Subversive! Communist church! Die! Smelling kaffir! Swine! Skunk! Political donkey! Will you speak? Will you speak? Will you speak?" Stop. Dead silence. No move-ment. One frightening, long minute.

"Window! Let the dirty swine see the bowels of the earth. If we can-not get anything out of his live body, we shall get something out of his corpse." The officer moved from the window.

The two whites, now joined by a black, grabbed me, dangled me upside down through the window, and demanded, "Amalgamation! Amalgamation! Botswana! Botswana boys! If we cannot get a satisfac-tory answer, we will let you fall to the ground below, breaking your spinal

---

[2]The South African government suspected that several black political groups were coming together.

[3]They were accusing me of recruiting schoolboys to go to Botswana to the liberation movement.

cord and scattering your cheeky brains all over the place, and we'll tell the world that you jumped through the window."

Thank God I had been fasting since Thursday, for a full stomach would have added weight to the hopelessness of the situation. I said a prayer at that moment. I could even afford to speak softly and move my lips. My mouth was at a safe distance, though my life as a whole was in danger. "If I must hang in the air, Lord, let it be. Your Son hung on the cross. Who am I to be identified with his suffering! What an honor! Your Son suffered to regain the life—the rights of all people enslaved and oppressed by death and the devil. He died for the whole world."

"Now, kaffir, are you ready to tell the truth if we pull you in?"

"Oh Lord, I am only one of many in South Africa who must hang for the liberation and freedom and rights of the oppressed whose only wrong is their skin, painted by you. If I must die, let it be; but one thing I ask of you, let not the hope for freedom die in my people. Amen."

Once the window-on-the-bowels-of-the-earth exercise was over, the officer in charge demanded that I tell about the underground activities of all black organizations, banned and unbanned, of my church activities, of the SACC, SASO, the CI, the Bold Evangelical Christian Organization (BECO), the Lutheran World Federation, the escape routes to Botswana, Lesotho, Swaziland, Mozambique. He demanded to know my personal and family history; he wanted me to write down all the sermons I had preached and all the speeches I had ever delivered. Yes, he demanded to know my connections with trade unions, my involvement in student riots, and all about other connections. When all my verbal answers could not satisfy them (I was all the time forced to stand), they handcuffed me, having made sure to place newspapers round my wrists to prevent visible marks, forced my legs through my arms, and pushed a stick in between, placing it on two high chairs. And there I was, hanging in the air. The pains were indescribable. The black bully disappeared, followed by the two white bullies and finally by their leader.

I was the loneliest man in the world. Next door I could hear the white giant: "Take off your dress. Your smelling petticoat. Show us your terrorist thing which makes your terrorist boyfriends go mad." There was a struggle. Some thuds. The walls shook. Silence, very uncomfortable silence. Heavy breathing, staccato pace. Another struggle. Then, "She's trying to bite me. Bring those pliers. We shall pull her thing out." A long, long struggle. How could a young girl, judging by her voice, keep these white giants and the black bully struggling? It sounded like the Third World War. Like the superpowers allied against tiny Lesotho.

"NO. No. NO. Ngiafa baba! Ngiyafa baba [I'm dying, Daddy]! NO. NO . . . NO . . . " For some time her screams had miraculously healed my pains. When her screams subsided, I had started groaning, and when nothing could be heard from her, I continued exactly where she had left off. For the first time in twenty years I cried like a young girl, letting loose all the tears that had been clogged for years by the artificial pride of masculinity. I was actually surprised when Thick Bully shouted a message to Thin Bully (as I came to call the two bullies), Kerels, kom julle hoor; hy kraai soos'n haan ("Chaps, come, hear; he crows like a cock"). I had thought I was cackling like a hen. All four were back in my room. Each took a can of beer from a small refrigerator, and as if responding to the movements of a choir conductor, they opened the cans at the same time, drank at the same pace, and emptied the cans as if a voice had shouted, "Stop." In a chorus they shouted, "Are you going to speak? Speak the truth! Nothing but the truth! Stop telling lies in this room of truth [*waarkamer* or *waarheidkamer*]."

I agreed that I would tell the truth, hoping I would be let off the hook. I was wrong. "First you must tell the truth on the cross; thereby we shall know that you can tell the truth on the floor." Having said this, the white giant let the group out, but before he closed the door, he said, "Some friendly advice to my dean: Arrange all your facts concerning all our questions in order to tell them all without explanation in five minutes. Remember, we cannot free you, only the truth can make you free. You are a man of the Bible, you should know that." This time my silent pain had the upper hand over the screams in the adjoining offices, the rooms known as truth rooms when interrogations were in session. Again I was alone, and lonely. . . except for the uncompromising pain. I arranged my screams in a meaningful chorus, directed at a real target, clothed in the words of Calvary, in Hebrew and Aramaic, in Venda and in Sotho: Eli, Eli, lama sabachtani! Eloi, Eloi, lama sabachtani! Mudzimu wanga wo ntutshelani! Modimo waka O nthogeletseng! ("My God, my God, why have you forsaken me?"). My God! My God! Never in my life had these words been so meaningful.

When I regained consciousness only the black fellow was in the room. "Welcome to the land of the living, black brother. Do you remember me? Sit up and look at me properly." I had only leg irons. The stick and the handcuffs had been removed, leaving rings of blood on my wrists and ankles. At one stage or another the newspaper slips must have moved, allowing direct contact between iron and flesh. The face before me was familiar. I had seen it at many BPC and SASO conferences and seminars. Most recently I had seen him at Sibasa during student riots. Near

Sibasa police station he had stopped to greet me, raised a clenched fist and shouted, "Power to the people," to which I responded, "Power to Azania [South Africa]." He had then indicated, "The Soweto struggle continues and is even growing; how are you managing in this part of Azania? I must already say that we are very much impressed by your performance this side." When he uttered the last word, I was already more than three meters from him, so that he had to half-shout it. Here he was today, dressed as he was at Sibasa: blue jeans, a black afro-shirt with a clenched fist on the breast and a map of Africa on the back with the word "Azania" on the southern tip, smart boots, their color lost in dirt, unaccompanied by socks. His hair was like dusty wild grass, long, uncombed, and uncared for.

"Now, brother," he added in faltering Venda, "I have been one of you. I can assure you that we are fighting a stupid war, a lost cause. I am now several years with the security police. I enjoy my job. I have seen the light. During my many years of service all the political die-hards that we detained ultimately cracked like nuts under pressure. Some, within minutes of detention, on their own initiative would say, 'I want to tell you now. I will not wait for interrogation.' They would sing like birds. Others crack after an hour, a day or two, a week or a month, even more, but one principle is clear: they all crack sooner or later. No person can carry the Drankensberg[4] and survive. Now you should make up your mind: tell all with the minimum of suffering or spill all the beans in the bottom of hell. Perhaps you should know," he went on, "that your friends were also detained immediately after you. For the past two weeks we have been working on them. We now know all about you. We also know that you were influenced and misled. We do not want to punish you, but those who misguided you to misguide other people who in turn misguided other people, particularly the young. I do not want to see the white police deal with you again. You are mine, but only if you cooperate, if you play ball. It is now one in the morning. They come back at eight. Here is a pen and some paper. Let the river flow, do not dam it up, let it burst and carry you into the ocean. Good luck, black brother, do a good job."

I sat on a comfortable chair, table and stationery before me. The most distasteful task stared me in the eyes. I tackled the bull by the horns. I wrote and wrote, and wrote and wrote and wrote and wrote and wrote. Every time I filled a page, he would take the leaf for examination. "You should improve your details. Names of persons, places, dates, motives,

---

[4]The largest mountain range in South Africa.

things minuted and unminuted, who proposed what motion, who seconded, who opposed—all these things must come in." I wrote . . . and . . . wrote . . . for hours on end. Before he left, at about eight in the morning, I overheard him say to the whites who had just arrived, "The dean has written a lot of rubbish. It is lying on the table."

Two bullies marched in, a completely new lot. The one walked behind me and landed a deafening hot punch on my right ear. Simultaneously the other removed the chair from under me, shoved me to the ground, and kicked the table over me. Another kick, this time to my groin, followed by another, three . . . five . . . innumerable. A hundred pages of statement lay scattered all over the floor. I was forced to stand up, but halfway, a blow to my face left me tumbling backwards. One bully put his boot on my neck while the other placed his boot on my genitals. I was allowed to stand, and then forced to carry the "liberation stick," with weights attached to both ends. Carrying this stick with hands raised, I was forced to jump into the air without rest, singing loudly, "Amandla Awethu! Power to the people! Power to Azania!" I sweated like a horse and groaned like a hungry pig. Totally exhausted, I let the stick fall on the floor and collapsed. Heaving like a heavyweight boxer in the fifteenth round, I managed to mumble a few words, syllable by syllable: "I . . . am . . . tired . . . I . . . am . . . dying."

The same officer from hours before, the white giant, had arrived in the meantime and instructed that cold water be poured over my head. I managed to gulp two or three mouthfuls, mixed with dirty, salty sweat. But who cared? I was helped into a standing position, and then forced to sit on an "imaginary chair," that is, to squat, arms stretched to the sides, unsupported.

My energy exhausted, I collapsed. They kicked . . . pummeled . . . rolled and spat on me. They pulled me up on my knees, supporting me on both sides. I collapsed.

When I regained consciousness I was being treated by a white doctor. "Why are you sweating?" the doctor inquired. Before I could say a word, the security policeman said, "He is just excited."

The doctor gave me some medicines and then said in Afrikaans, Hy is baie swak; hy mag vrek; moenie hom harde oefening gee nie ("He is too weak; he may die; do not give him hard exercise"). After his departure, the interrogation continued. I had to stand the whole time.

Next came the "liberation broom," a very broad, heavy broom. I was forced to sweep aimlessly in the room. In the process I would now get a hard kick from behind, a surprise punch below the belt, another on the chest or stomach, then on the head, or a chop at the back of the neck. It had already been two days with no food, and no sleep. No water, no rest, no peace, no love, no sense, no mercy. . . perhaps no God. Several times I would fall asleep standing, only to be awakened by a hot slap that sent me flying across the room.

Occasionally the white giant would pretend to be very friendly, saying, "Stop your nonsense, you youngsters. This man is a pastor. You need not be rough with him. He will cooperate." Then he would command me to sit on the floor. "Do you have any confessions to make?" When my answer did not satisfy him, he would jump in fury. "You kaffirs are stupid. An adult kaffir does not even have the brains of a five-year-old white child. Yet you say you do not want Bantu education. If you are doing so badly in Bantu education already, how do you think you will manage with the white man's education?" I wrote and wrote. And wrote. And wrote and wrote and wrote and wrote and wrote. And wrote. "You continue to write all this rubbish, and you will see what will happen to you. You and Steve Biko have corrupted the youth of this country. You preach that apartheid is the policy of the devil and that those who practice this policy are agents of the devil. We want to tell you once and for all, if we must choose between sharing power with nonwhites or obliterating them, we shall choose the latter. If you do not like apartheid, you'd better pack your bags and be off to Tanzania to live with your communist brothers." After this lecture the officer went through my statement, popularly known as a "confession." A tall, slender white man came in, most probably senior to all present. They all stood up and saluted him. The white giant greeted him, "Good afternoon, Major." "Afternoon, Captain. But why does this baboon not stand up? Is this what you are teaching him, giving him soft porridge[5] just because he is a bloody pastor? Laat hy gaan kak [Let him (expletive deleted)]. He is smelling terribly. Take him out of this office; it is not a pig sty!"

I was led out by both security policemen, to some holding cells nearby. "Come out, madala!" one called out contemptuously. Out came an old man, as pale as a ghost, lips cracked, and apparently very weak physically. "Do you know this man, madala [*madala* means "old man"]?" Instead of responding to the question, the man raised a clenched fist and saluted me: "Power to the people. Power, brother! You are fine. I am fine. Power!" I knew him. I recognized him—once we were both guest speakers at a student conference in Wilgespruit—old man Muthuping. Some call him Justice.

---

[5]Light treatment.

Soon we marched back to the "room of truth." Kick-Bully (he earned this designation) said, "I hope you have now seen what we are capable of." Back in the room, the interrogation continued. Toward the close of the third day, a young black detainee was brought into the torture room, unmanacled, unleg-ironed, as free as a hare in a fowl run. I recognized his face but did not remember his name. When asked whether he knew me, he readily answered, "Yes. He is Farisani," and then disappeared. "He is walking around freely," said the white giant, "a privilege you may also receive, provided you tell the truth, the whole truth."

By now I was exhausted, very thirsty, very hungry, and very sleepy. My statement, or confession, was still unacceptable. The police still demanded something terroristic, communistic, and subversive in my confession. Anything which proved my innocence and my friends' innocence was not welcome. I must say it is at this stage that lies crop into many a so-called confession. For pure survival, to avoid more torture, one tends to embellish one's statements to gratify the sadistic nature of one's interrogators. I did not pass this juncture unscarred.

After expressing much skepticism, the officer instructed one of the white fellows to "take the rotten kaffir to the shower, to wash his rotten ass and smelly clothes." As the handcuffs and leg irons were removed in preparation for the shower, the officer added, "If he attempts something funny, let him run a few meters and then send him to kaffir heaven."

I washed my clothes, without soap. I hung them on the fence to dry. After three hours they were only half dry, but I willingly put them on when instructed to do so, for since my childhood I had never sat naked for three hours. As we walked past one "room of truth," the door stood ajar, and there I saw a naked girl, handcuffed and leg-ironed, in a pool of water. One look was enough.

Two black lackeys drove me back to Pietermaritzburg prison, always speaking between themselves as if I did not exist. Only at one stage did one of them say, "Those bosses admire your stand for the truth and your readiness to suffer for your convictions." In response I told them that I was very hungry, and needed something to eat. "We cannot buy you anything. They shout at us just as they shout at you. You should have told the bosses. We are very sorry; we cannot help you."

Back to Square One

"God, I have suffered the most horrible things imaginable. Just have one look at me! What do you think? For many years I have preached that you are almighty, but in prison you are all-powerless; I told the congregations that you are a savior, yet you cannot save me; that you have ears, yet you do not hear my prayers; that you have eyes, yet you do not see my plight. God, do you really exist? Frankly I now doubt your very existence, your very being. How does one explain these tortures in a world in which God is said to be in charge? Honestly, unless you prove otherwise, I see no way in which I can again preach to the congregations to believe in you. You will do well to remember, Lord, that it is not my duty to discover you but your duty to reveal yourself to me, here or never. Amen." I was not sure whether anybody, human or divine, did hear my prayer. I was just happy that I prayed. The next morning I realized that my Bible was left at Howick. During those frantic moments it never occurred to me that I had brought a Bible along. The security police had been correct in their predictions.

During exercise time I got the shock of my life. As I ran in circles some detainees whispered loudly whenever I passed under their windows: Umfundisi! Umfundisi! ("Pastor! Pastor!"). They knew me. They also knew that I am a pastor, a man of God. Detention or no detention, I was still a man of God, a pastor. It gave me great joy just to know that even in my suffering I could still bring joy to my fellow sufferers. A sign of hope in a situation of total despair and helplessness.

When I eventually was allowed a Bible by the Gideons (later I also got mine back through untiring appeals to the magistrate who came once a fortnight), I would prepare sermons for my neighboring cellmates, for the congregations at home, and for myself. I shouted my sermons at the top of my voice, especially on Sundays, and rejoiced greatly whenever the other detainees would respond with an "Allelujah, amen." I had made a collection of choruses in Venda, Zulu, Sotho, English, Hebrew, and Shangaan, which I listed at the back of my Revised Standard Version, along with the hymns that I could remember. I sang when my spirits were high and also during times of unspeakable depression. One thing that never passed through my mind, even for a moment, was suicide. I had vowed that despite terrible tortures, I would never do their dirty job for them. They would have to strangle, suffocate, or hang me. They would have to push me through the window. Not only do my principles prevent me from killing another person, I may also not touch my own life—God's life—even if I were to remain alive, tortured without end. Better that I should make false confessions, which I could later retract, than take away life, which no man can restore.

I habitually fasted from Thursday or Friday until Sunday, my regimen culminating with Holy Communion on Sunday. I did the liturgy from memory, and used maize and water for bread and wine respectively. Never before in my life did the death of the Lord mean so much to me.

I also had a daily prayer list that included police, government, church, religious organizations, all continents, our Devhula/Leboa circuit, individuals, the sick, the healthy, the poor, detainees, prisoners, torturers, and murderers. I must admit that the first time I ever prayed seriously for the security police and the government was when I was in prison. Only then did I realize how much they need our daily, serious-minded intercessions; whoever reads this book with a sympathetic attitude will be forced to pray for them at the turn of every page.

I enjoyed the visits by the magistrate, not so much because of their usefulness as because they served to break the loneliness. After all, who would dare complain about torture when the magistrate is always in the company of police, even the security police? What is more, the police make no bones about the consequences of giving distasteful reports to magistrates. Before the real magistrate comes, the security police often do their rounds disguised as magistrates; cursed is the detainee who "tells nonsense." In all fairness, it is actually impossible to tell who is a genuine magistrate and who is a fraud. It is better to play it safe. I for one always limited my complaints to the lack of sufficient blankets, the quality and quantity of food, the lack of a Bible (when it was left at Howick), and ill health (of course, to tell of the causes would be suicidal). Very often my requests were derided as wild demands and my ill health as detention psychosis, but in some instances the magistrate was very helpful. He got my Bible back, and a second Bible was provided by the Gideons. I got additional blankets and a second mat, and was allowed one half loaf of bread and one half liter of milk every fortnight (at times, every week), the cost of which was deducted from my pocket money, still in the custody of the police since the night of my detention.

The Silence Is Broken

Up till now the god of Pretoria had the upper hand. He dictated my food, my bedding, my sleep, my sitting and standing, my exercise, my cleanliness, my company, my day and night. My very existence was a matter of his grace. *My* heavenly Father was for all intents and purposes dead—unhearing, unseeing, uncaring, unconcerned, unloving, unlike his being. One evening I knocked on the door of God's grave: "God, are you able to protect and preserve? Perhaps I should read you Psalms 22, 91, and 121. Let me also read you Matt. 11:28–30; 7:7–10; and 2 Peter 5:6ff. There you are: the promises are yours, not mine. It is up to you to live up to your promises. Amen."

That night I had a vision. I was caught in a great storm. Dust and stones overwhelmed me. A mighty force carried me into the air. I could see the storm far beneath me, and also police who tried in vain to hit me with stones. Their stones either fell short of the target or were deflected by the force of the strong wind. When the vision came to an end, I was very excited, though not convinced. I pleaded, "God, if this vision is from you, let me have a second one, for nothing is impossible with you."

In the second vision I saw myself walking on a gravel road. Two white snakes came from nowhere. They stood on their tails, one to my right and another to my left, reaching above my head. Both tried to bite me at the center of the head, but an unseen power made both feeble, the two collapsing to either side. Then I heard a voice say, "Behold, I give unto you power to tread on serpents and scorpions, and over all the powers of the enemy: and nothing shall by any means hurt you" (Luke 10:19). I reached for my Bible at the end of this vision. I walked to the door, trying to make use of the ray of light that filtered into the cell, but without success. Cursed be those who control the light from outside. When light came in, the next morning, I had already been waiting for what felt like decades. Like a man possessed, I paged through the New Testament, and when I finally fixed my eyes on Luke 10:19, I wondered whether I was still in charge of my five senses. I prayed. I sang. I made spontaneous poems and recited them. I put my Bible under my arm and danced to the chorus "The B-i-b-l-e. Yes, that's the book for me. I stand alone on the word of God, the B-i-b-l-e." Again:

> The best book to read is the Bible
> The best book to read is the Bible
> If you read it everyday, it will lead you on your way
> The best book to read is the Bible.

In answer to my further prayers the Lord said to me, "You are not alone in opposing apartheid. Blacks say it is wrong. The church of God all over the world says it is wrong. The Organisation of African Unity says the same. So does the United Nations. God-fearing people say apartheid is wrong."

"But Lord, the security police have said during the torture sessions that I am a child of the devil, that anybody who opposes apartheid cannot be from God, since the government of South Africa is God's government doing God's will. They even told me that, should they kill me, I would march straight into hell. Of course, I do not believe them, but at times I have doubts. . . ." In the next vision I saw many horses, at the second coming of the Son of man, entering New Jerusalem. On the back of each was a placard with names of the saved. My name was also among the many.

I was still unsatisfied, unconvinced, doubting: "God, give me a last vision, please? I want to be sure that my mind is not misleading me. Is it true that my friends have lied against me and that my family is starving, as the police claim?" In the answering vision, I saw my friends walking scot-free at home, and my house full of food of all kinds. The police had definitely told lies. Thus says the Lord.

Then in the next few days the screams increased at night. I "accidentally" saw some detainees lying in the cells leg-ironed and handcuffed, in pools of ice-cold water. I regularly met naked and half-naked detainees on my way to or from exercise. At night I could hear and partially see through the window how naked black bodies walked on sharp stones and nails, and how the car engines were kept on, either to drown the screams or to provide electric shocks to the exposed victims. I became so scared I sought refuge in prayer. "God, once more please. Just for the last time. Do again assure me of your protection. I cannot stand these things any longer." Before I concluded my prayer I was carried into the air. There were angels beneath me, above me, on my sides. They moved in waves, and with every move they went higher, and I with them. When all was over, I fell on my knees: "Lord, I am assured of your concern, care, love, and protection. You may as well send all your other angels to protect the other detainees and the people at home. I need only one." At Howick I was a broken and defeated man. Now God had turned everything into victory. Where my cleverness and personal courage had crumbled, God raised up divine wisdom and endurance. Whereas I had been a spiritual, emotional, and physical wreck, God had resurrected me to a new life and a new hope. My extremity had become God's opportunity. God's power became visible in weakness. For the first time I came to know some of the things that differentiate human beings from God. Where my church leaders and lawyers could be of little use, God became available. Where my friends could not reach me, God could. I had been taken up the mountain of temptation: "Why suffer all these things, Dean? If only you would cooperate, you would be a great man in Venda." But I had been saved by a soft, tender voice: "No man can serve two Lords; you cannot serve God and mammon." And again, "For whosoever will save his life shall lose it; but whosoever shall lose his life for my sake and the gospel's, the same shall save it . . ." (Mark 8:35–38). Better that I should be a nobody in the arms of God than a great man in the diabolical arms of apartheid. It was comforting to know I was innocent, that I was right. It was comforting to be aware of God's active presence.

God's intervention did not mean the disappearance of all problems. My teeth got rotten, and I spent many sleepless nights because of toothache. It was also very frustrating not to know when one's turn of torture would come and when one would possibly be released, if ever. Medical treatment was hopelessly inadequate. Usually large white pills were dealt out by the police for all kinds of sicknesses. At times the cells were raided and personal articles strewn all over the cell. No explanation or apology was given after the act. This only helped to aggravate the detainees' feelings of helplessness and total exposure.

April: Mini-Howick

My next interrogation came when I was collected in the night of April 20, 1977. It lasted through the twenty-second of the month. This time it was done somewhere in Pietermaritzburg. For me it was a little less intense than I had experienced at Howick, but for two or three other detainees it was much worse than Howick. One prisoner, I discovered, had spent three weeks without food and water, and could hardly speak, not to mention walk. Another was screaming in the *waarkamer,* hanging upside down. Later on, the youthful whites rushed into my *waarkamer* and announced to their senior, who was cross-questioning me on my "confession" and on documents collected from my house on the day I was detained, "He is now talking. He is singing like a bird!" The colonel in charge nodded approval and said, "We hope our pastor will not have to come to you. Up till now there's no need." During this three-day interrogation session I was allowed to catch a few moments of sleep, and to have some food and water. The torture recipe was the same as at Howick, but of less intensity and duration. This more relaxed atmosphere gave me opportunity to retract many lies that I had vomited under pressure at Howick. I had, for example, "admitted" that the church and the Bold Evangelical Christian Organisation are political fronts, when I knew this to be the worst nonsense in the world. Retracting fake statements was the most strenuous process, since the police kept on threatening me with further torture: "We shall not hesitate to take you back to Howick if you keep on withdrawing your confessions. Do not be misled by our friendly attitude."

The Lord in Action

Back in the cell, the Lord showed me in a vision how I crossed a flooded river and how my friends did the same without being swept away. In another vision, the Lord showed how I managed to put out a large fire that was threatening to consume me. Encouraged by all these visions, I started to sing loudly in praise of God, and the other detainees joined. "You shall stop this inflammatory music, or else . . . ," threatened a policeman who was apparently listening in for a long time. Full of courage, I poured my heart out for him: "You have taken away all my rights. I cannot move; I cannot serve my church; I cannot have fellowship; I have no access to a lawyer, to my bishop or anybody. Now you want to deny me my last right—my right to praise the Lord. No, I shall continue to sing." The police threatened drastic measures, which, however, never materialized.

Assured of God's response, I decided to put my personal and religious problems to the Lord. First, I received an answer on baptism and on my ministry. Second, I received an answer about my marital future. I had three ladies in mind as possible life partners. When the vision came, only two were in line. First in line was Miss I Love You above All. Second in line was Regina. Their positions were changed: Regina came to the front while my Miss First came second. She finally disappeared behind Regina. There alone, unrivaled, stood Regina Mudzunga Nemaembeni. From that moment I knew who would be my wife, and although I never used this vision, or others that followed, in our discussions after my release, I always felt assured that Reggy would be my wife. When we finally agreed to marry, we discovered, as we shared openly thereafter, that the Lord had spoken to both of us. In gratitude to God for revelations that I had in prison and that we both had concerning our relationship, we decided to call our first daughter Ndzumbululo (that is, "revelation"). Her younger sister is named Ndamulelo Mbofholowo ("redemption, freedom").

Because I had no toothpaste or toothbrush, my teeth continued to deteriorate. When, after many complaints, a dentist eventually came, he mainly succeeded in breaking two of my teeth, since he did not have proper equipment for the job. He suggested to the police that they take me to Edendale Hospital. It took about two weeks of hard and sleepless nights of pain before the Lord revealed to me in a vision that I would be taken to hospital. The Lord was correct: the following day I found myself in hospital in spite of my little faith in the revelations. After this I was allowed to buy a toothbrush and toothpaste. I was very grateful, although this was more than a month too late. Later I also received a parcel of clothes from home, although I was not informed from whom it came. This signaled an end to the naked sessions that were a necessity whenever I had to wash my clothes.

The Final Lap

The final interrogation session lasted from May 19 through May 24. It was extraordinarily friendly. I spent my nights in the cell and was interrogated only during the day. The food was first class: eggs, toasted bread, coffee or tea with milk, rice, beef, milk, meat pies, hamburgers—

all things that one gets in a five-star hotel. This hospitality scared me to the marrow. What would follow?

Every night the Lord revealed to me things relating to the following day's interrogation: the looks and size of the interrogation room, the faces of the people who would be involved in the interrogation, what questions they would ask and the motives behind them. The next day everything was as the Lord had revealed. When the first question came, I looked at the interrogator, "Here is a man who thinks he is very clever. He probably thinks he has taken me by surprise. If only he knew the power of the Lord!" I could not have it. I asked to go answer the call of nature leg-ironed. I was escorted to the toilet by a lackey. Once inside, I released only tears . . . and tears and tears. "O, Lord, when I asked you to help me, when I begged for your intervention, I did not ask for this much. Your greatness overwhelms me. Your miracles embarrass me." When the police became impatient, I flushed a quantity of nothingness down the sewage system and wiped away my tears.

The last sessions of interrogation became a mysterious combination of hope, fear, confusion, despair. "Dean, do not be embarrassed by the leg irons. We want to prevent suicides." (But your people nearly killed me at Howick, I thought.) "Make no mistake. The government has all the power. Lawyers and the church are nothing. Even if your lawyer or bishop sees you now through the window, he cannot help you. The power is in our hands. Working with the government means security and safety. Look at Africa. Communism, starvation, and suffering are everywhere. If you were opposing the government outside South Africa, you would be dead by now. Bantu education is good. Look how clever you are. You are better off than many Africans in Malawi, Lesotho, Nigeria—than anywhere else in Africa. The other day you said Beyers Naude is God's prophet. I cannot deny it. But I am not sure. Perhaps you are one too. As for me, I have to do this work for my family. We do not persecute people; we do not like sending youngsters to Robben Island. But we do not like subversion. We are not worried about this BPC-SASO nonsense. You only have to learn your lesson. We say in Afrikaans, Wat jy saai gaan maai jy ["One must learn one's lesson; you reap what you sow"]. Sign here, on every page. Your future and life are in my hands. By the way do you know the people in these photos?"

"NO. No. No. No. Yes. Why? No. No. No. No. No. No. No. Perhaps. Why? No. No."

"Thank you, Dean. I am now sending you back to your hotel for another ten months. We shall first interrogate all your friends and then come back to you. Good luck. Good stay." With these words, the colonel had sealed my fate. Or so I thought.

A Small Seed of Love

The last time I saw one of my torturers was May 24. On that day he had looked away from me, although I had hoped to exchange a smile, a small seed of love in a world of murder and hatred.

I was in my cell, away from good food and police fellowship. Now I was back in the company of screamers, of gray-faced ghosts whose future lay fixed in their despair, a world of dim lights and no sun. Had I come away from near death to nearer death? To drive away these thoughts, I would daily, at times three times a day, clean my cell until I was convinced it was the cleanest cell in the world. I crawled on my knees, cleaning up all pieces of wool from the mats or blankets, even my hair. By this time I had a small cloth that I utilized to good effect. I had come to love my cell. It was my home, my only home . . . my life, my death, my hope, my all.

Moments of frustration would often cloud all sense of joy. Why should I stay in prison for a further ten months? "Lord, why did you make me a prophet to call out loudly [Isaiah 58; 59]? Why do you leave me in the devil's power [Psalm 22]? Why can you not fulfill your promises [Psalms 118; 119]? Why not kill me yourself?" For days I screamed and rolled and kicked and protested and fasted and rebelled and blasphemed and thanked and cried. God would always defeat me into repentance, prayer, and singing. Eventually I said, "God, if you still want me to learn of your greatness, keep me in prison as much as you like. It can only be to my own good and to the good of my church."

Let My Tortured Child Go

Frankly, I did not enjoy the prospect of staying in prison for ten months, even if I liked the idea of growing spiritually. It was June 3, 1977. Perhaps it was already midnight. In a vision, I saw police opening my cell. They asked if I was Farisani. I said yes. "Take your clothes, all your things, for today you are going home." At the entrance I rejoiced when the police told the man in charge, "Remove his name from your register, he is going home." Still in the vision, I was led to the charge office. I was given back my watch and belt, and shown a white paper with financial figures. What does this mean? A bribe? We drove to the main interrogation center. Then to Johannesburg in a large car. On the way the driver asked me whether I had a driver's license. Upon my answering in the positive, he asked me to drive, since he was tired. I was not shown in the vision how I traveled to Beuster, my home. On arrival at

Beuster, I was met by many people, among whom were two people I knew were in detention, since they were detained before me.

When the vision ended I became very angry with God. How could God be so cruel? Why should he flatter me? Why should he play with my mind? Though the previous visions came true, how could this one materialize? Had the police not told me that I would stay in prison ten months hence? The police, not God, had the prison keys. Very often I had asked God to open the prison doors. He would not. He could not. Why should he now, all of a sudden, promise this possibility?

Very early in the morning I walked around in circles singing choruses I had made up. I felt a mixture of joy and sorrow, hope and frustration. The door opened, the police stood before me. "Are you Dean Farisani?"

"Yes sir," I responded.

"Take your clothes. All your things, you are going home," he said. It was too good to be true. As far as I was concerned, it was not reality but the continuation of the previous night's vision. In the charge office the woman behind the counter gave me my watch and belt and some money, saying, "This is the balance of the money you deposited with us. We have deducted the money you used for toothbrush, toothpaste, soap, bread, and milk." Henceforth all things happened as the Lord had predicted. After I had turned down the lieutenant's offer to help drive, on the grounds that I had been too long in prison and thus could not trust my reflexes, he said to me, "If you find very old cars, do contact me at Springs. My hobby is collecting old cars. I am prepared to pay, provided the price is not unreasonably high." Till today I have not found him a single old car. In Johannesburg the lieutenant bought me a third-class ticket and bade me farewell. Now, the third-class coaches are often over-crowded and dangerous. So I went to Soweto and borrowed money to buy a second-class ticket.

The next day I arrived in Louis Trichardt. The police in Pietermaritz-burg had told me to ask the police in Louis Trichardt for transport to Beuster. I did not. I wanted to reach my home. What guarantee did I have that I would not be locked up again in Louis Trichardt? In fact I had even refused to carry the books, sermons, and documents that the police had taken when I was detained. I said I would collect them by car later. What guarantee did I have that I would not be detained for having the same documents, at the checkpoints on the roads leading home? On arrival at Beuster I was welcomed by many people, among them Aubrey Mokoena, who was detained before me. Only now did I come to know that he had been released some time before me. The tortured child was free, back at Beuster, back in the circuit—free for a while.

A day later a reporter of the *Daily Mail* phoned me: "How are you?"

I said, "I am safe and healthy in body and mind." I had been thoroughly warned that should I tell "nonsense" to the newspapers, I would be paid back in full measure.

A Nine Days' Wonder

I cherished my freedom, every minute of it. South Africa, however, was still the same; apartheid spat straight into my face at every corner of life. For how long would I manage to keep quiet?

Friends can be a disappointment, particularly those one loves most. During my detention one friend stayed in my house, in my bedroom, and left a lot of empty beer cans there. He imported girlfriends into my house. Some misused the food given to my mother and orphaned cousins. Some Christian brothers and sisters did nothing to help. Some trusted friends disappeared into thin air. A few came to apologize, others to explain why they failed to help. Many more never came.

The widespread students' strikes that erupted first in Soweto on June 16, 1976, were still on. The previous week I had appealed to both the authorities and the students to sit down and talk it over. "The problem of Bantu education cannot be solved by shooting and clubbing our children into silence. Let us talk it over," I said in my sermon on October 16. I did not know then that this would be my last sermon in 1977.

SECOND TIME IN
THE BOWELS OF

HELL

October 21, 1977. I had just visited Duthuni Congregation with one elder, to encourage them in their harvest collections. On our way back, in my Ford Ranchero, I decided to buy a newspaper at Sibasa. The manager of the shop said to me, "Many people are being detained. We hope this time they do not touch our dean." Five minutes later, at the junction of Patrick Mphephu and De Wet Nel Streets, a policeman stopped me and directed me into the police station. My short treasured freedom was a nine days' wonder. I was, in the charge office, given a warrant of arrest in Afrikaans. It was signed by a Venda minister of justice, a member of my church and of our men's league. In the cell I found two detainees, a magistrate's clerk and a watchmaker. Later we were joined by the evangelist Phineas Phosiwa. His story made us laugh uncontrollably: "When the police came, they asked me to go with them to fetch the dean's car. On the way, one of them said, 'Is Phosiwa not on our detention list?' 'He is,' answered another."

Before we slept in our dirty cell in dirty blankets on smelly mats, we were joined by an inspector of schools, an old man of sixty-four. "Where is the bed?" he asked. We all laughed. Beds? In prison?

During the night and the following days we were joined by many more: teachers, clerks, principals of schools, businessmen, students, all sorts. In our small cell we numbered seventeen. Later we learned that all the police stations were full in Venda. The following week our group was transferred to Louis Trichardt, guarded by police with R1 Army rifles. On our arrival, the white policemen called us cockroaches, bedbugs, school burners, terrorists— any dirty word that came their way. "Today you will taste white power!" they shouted. We slept in a large cell. The blankets were completely infested with lice. The next day we were moved into unventilated cells in three groups. In our cell, there were six of us. We were packed in tightly. Sweat flowed like water, even on the walls. The light was always on. At lunchtime, we were served with very hot food. There was no privacy. When one wanted to use the toilet, some closed their eyes while others looked at the wall. In the evening we pleaded with the police, and all seventeen of us were transferred to a larger cell. This cell had a common shower, under which we all washed ourselves, the sixteen-year-old, and the sixty-four-year-old, each before all. The food was relatively decent. Exercise time was given, ranging between thirty minutes and one hour a day, depending on the mood of the policeman in charge. One lackey, a sergeant, was very impolite, particularly in the presence of the whites. Some whites were polite, others very rude. On one occasion, for medical inspection we were made to stand in a line, our trousers unzipped, our privates peeping. One of us suffered from frightening epileptic fits. During these attacks he needed fresh air. We would shout that the door should be opened, but with little success. We did bring our complaints to a magistrate, who looked very friendly but achieved very little.

During the following week we were joined by a second group, who occupied an adjacent cell. Some of them had been badly beaten up. This group often accused one another of being informers, something our group was lucky to avoid, although some alleged that a certain young man pushed out notes above the door every night.

Two weeks later we were transferred to Pietersburg, only the seventeen, now known as the Great Seventeen. On our arrival, one policeman covered in buttons and medals of all sorts warned us, "If you behave like gentlemen, we shall treat you like gentlemen; if not, we shall not." We all got brand-new blankets, towels, soaps, and mats.

The showers were in cubicles and ran both cold and warm water. On request we were given a brand new Afrikaans Bible and were allowed to hold services, provided we moderated our voices. Every day we had a solid one-hour exercise time. The police were very friendly, unusually polite, both whites and blacks. We were allowed to write letters home in English or Afrikaans. The food was, to make a very long story short, excellent. Medical attention was quick and thorough.

This treatment in Pietersburg was extraordinary. There was no interrogation, except for a few students. None of our group was tortured. Later we learned that our group was meant to be a showpiece for the International Red Cross team that had indicated it would visit South Africa. The Great Seventeen would have been presented to this team in Pietersburg.

When the authorities learned that they would not come, we were pushed back into the world of prison reality.

When we were transferred back to Sibasa after two weeks, I was appointed by the group to express our genuine thanks for the humane treatment. A few voices were against thanking police who detain innocent people. The leader of the police relished our thanks very much and asked us to do it in writing. We did not, for fear that our letter might be used to cover up other ill treatments of detainees. In fact, next to us there were people in solitary confinement, and although we appreciated the prayers by the prisoners every morning, we abhorred the curse words from the police that followed directly on the heels of the amen, just as they had in Louis Trichardt.

The change from Pietersburg back to Sibasa was dramatic, in a negative sense. One warder was downright rude. Food was horrible. Several times we had to drink water from the toilet. Occasionally we threw the food into the insatiable belly of Thizwilondi ("I do not care"), our faithful child, the toilet. The old man would always eat, even when the rest of the group fasted, saying, "I have to eat to keep flesh and soul together."

Colorful Moments

Our group enjoyed singing. Very often the prison walls shook with music. Even the police enjoyed our music. We were not allowed a Bible at Sibasa. We therefore selected some of the detainees to represent Matthew, Mark, Acts, Ephesians, etc. These were people who knew the Bible well. Whenever we would call on Matt. 5:9, the living Matthew would recite, "Blessed are the peacemakers, for they will be called children of God." On this we would then base our Bible studies for the day. In the cell was an area known as the pastor's corner; here I did all the counseling. Through this witness some accepted the Lord and backsliders were brought back to the Lord. We celebrated Holy Communion together. Using my Pietermaritzburg experience, I used porridge and water for the elements, reciting the liturgy from memory, not always perfectly.

We also managed to play many games, even boxing. At times arguments developed to uncontrollable levels, but not once was there ever a fight. Reconciliation was the highest principle. To pass time, we talked politics, told stories, and even discussed love affairs. Even the old gradually grew freer to talk of their love adventures, including the sixty-four-year-old. It was during these lonely moments that I broke the news that Regina and I were in love. It took many of them by surprise. They had already concluded that I was a confirmed bachelor. Some said openly that they would not imagine me embracing and kissing a woman. They fell on their backs in uncontrollable laughter when I told them that they were wrong.

Before Christmas we were allowed clothes and food parcels from home. Porridge and bread were sliced by the police before they were allowed in. Clothes were searched, both incoming and outgoing. Later we were allowed visitors once a week, relatives or sweethearts. The young women's visits were the high points for the young men. Usually we would listen to highly exaggerated reports, made easier by the fact that the meeting between the young couple took place under a tree, in the presence of a policeman but in our absence. Very often I suspected that some young men claimed to have met their young women whereas they were talking to their sisters or cousins. Ten minutes after one young man had claimed to have met his darling, a warder burst into the cell saying, "Come you, your brother is back again. He says he forgot to give you a message from your sick grandmother." We laughed our lungs out as the young man tried unsuccessfully to reconstruct his integrity.

When some of the seventeen were released in early January, 1978, we all had hoped to follow them. I was released on January 21, after ninety-three days in detention. "Farisani, Phosiwa, Makhari, Marema . . . pack your property. Go home." We were sorry to leave our friends but were consoled when after a few days they also were released. A number of students were tried in Pietersburg. Some of them ended up in Robben Island. As I write, they are there still. Others, we later learned, fled the country.

After I got home, I phoned the police. When they came I asked, "Why did you detain me? I want to know my crime lest I repeat it."

"I am not responsible for your detention," said the captain. "In fact I was surprised when I heard of your detention. As far as I am concerned you are innocent. This is why you are free. It was an emergency situation. People had to be detained. There was no time to investigate."

The captain concluded his speech and smiled. I looked into his face and said, "I am happy, not because you have said this to me but because God has heard what you said." We parted.

Homeland "Independence"

January 1978–November 1981. This was a period of traps, dangers, and horrible lies. Many people were detained after August 1978, particularly members of the Homeland Opposition Party. In addition they detained intellectuals, businessmen, foremen, students, magistrates, church leaders—all sorts of people. One critical word about the government or a chief during this time meant certain imprisonment. It was strongly rumored that one girl landed in detention for turning down the advances of a certain pro-government man.

When homeland elections took place, the Homeland Opposition Party won three out of four districts. Then Pretoria detained many of the newly elected members of parliament and intimidated the tribal chiefs. With the opposition out of the way, the elections for chief minister proceeded.

Being completely uninterested in homeland politics, I was not detained and thus had the privilege of listening to the statement of the white commissioner general of Venda, in the *South African English News:* "Today Vendaland has elected its chief minister. Venda is a great example to the whole of Africa as to what democracy means."

A day before "Venda independence" celebrations, I was asked to preach at the stadium. After consultations with the diocesan ministerial council I agreed to preach, provided I could choose my own text and my sermon was not to be censored. I preached about the foolish man who built his house on sand and the wise man who built on a rock. That night I was raided at home from 3 o'clock until 11:15 the next morning. My house was ransacked. I was banned from the rest of the program, and could not preach at any official function. Little did the authorities realize that I preached out of great love and not out of malice. I wanted to help the people, not flatter them with a gospel of peace when there was war raging at their very door. God be gracious unto them and let them know things that make for war and things that make for peace.

Then their attempts at entrapment began. I was baffled: young men came to me who wanted to "flee" the country. "Freedom fighters" came to me for help. Poor man of God! People tried to "sell" banned literature to me. When I could not buy for lack of money, they became generous and offered it free of charge. Mysterious cars with mysterious numbers tailed me day and night, at times blocking the road in formation, to cause an accident or force me to a halt. Several times I had to be escorted by congregants or fellow pastors. Once a black bakkie with iron bars welded to the front left its side of the road and headed straight for a head-on collision with me.

Only through God's grace did I manage, in a split second, to swerve onto the grass. Who was behind all this? I have no evidence. God will one day reveal the truth. Whether I live or die, no one can kill the truth. The most one can do is to confuse or distort the truth. One can delay the purposes of God, but no one can frustrate the will of the Lord.

Many lies were added to this recipe of traps. It was said that many dangerous nocturnal meetings were being held at Beuster, Pietersburg, Johannesburg, all over South Africa. I was said to be receiving salaries and cars from suspicious organizations (these were provided by the church). All sorts and sizes of lies. When finally my bishop and I made an appointment with the local authorities to discuss these problems, I was barred at the last minute from presenting our concerns. After this, the harassment continued, but thank God without success.

THIRD TIME IN
THE BOWELS OF

HELL

The Boiling Point

On the night of October 25, 1981, the Sibasa police station was bombed by guerrillas. Early that evening my wife, my brother-in-law, and his wife accompanied me to Louis Trichardt train station. When I boarded the train, there were at least two security policemen at the station. I did not know them then, but they did greet me. The next day I was in a suburb of Johannesburg, Rosettenville, attending a church council meeting. That afternoon someone told me about the attack, which he said he saw on television. I later bought the Johannesburg *Star,* and read the story. Since I was not in any way involved, either directly or indirectly, I had no reason to worry. Many people were later detained, among them Isaac Tshifhiwa Muofhe, a lay preacher in my church and a personal and family friend. I returned home and observed a heightened level of police activity in the whole area. On November 14, 1981, while at the Lutheran Theological College in Natal, I received a message that Isaac had died in detention. It was unbelievable. I drove the over one thousand kilometers back home with my wife and another couple. In Pietersburg and Louis Trichardt, agents provocateurs approached me to elicit my comments on Ike's death. I kept my cool. I later heard that the police had vowed to detain me should I go to make prayers to comfort the bereaved. It was November 15. I was dead scared. The next day I sat in the house paralyzed by fear until my wife came back from work. She is a teacher. I cupped her in my arms and kissed her. "Darling, enjoy your food and let us visit Lilian [Ike's widow]." My wife probably thought that I love her very much (which I surely do) and that I wanted to take her wherever I go. Little did she know that I was a cowardly dean, who desperately needed the support of a wife, a sort of minister of defense. Many times the voice of God had said to me, "You shall go." I always answered, "I will not. It is very dangerous. They will detain me. I will be killed. God, do not be reckless. I do not want a third detention." God never gave up. "If you are my pastor, not just a status-dean, you shall surely go." Later that afternoon we went. Lilian and Ike's mother were not there. We prayed with Lilian's mother. I took messages to other relatives. We discussed legal matters with lawyers in the evening. The next day, Tuesday the seventeenth, I did not go. On Wednesday the eighteenth, I went alone. I prayed with Lilian, and later with Ike's mother. I tried to comfort them. I was always very scared. Before I could jump away from this "dangerous spot," a certain young woman arrived, crying, "My husband has been badly tortured. He has been seen lying unconscious in hospital. Do everything to help me, Dean." I prayed with her and left. I met her relatives and called on one pastor. He was not at home. I left a message for him and drove home.

Boiling Masisi

They arrived fifteen minutes later, four security police. It was not necessary to announce their intentions. Everything was clear. But they did. "Dean, we have come to fetch you." My fearful hour had come.

"Where are you taking him?" Reggy wanted to know.

"To our offices," said the captain, contemptuously.

"When will you bring him back?" she asked.

"Perhaps today. If all goes well."

A visitor, Pastor Moremi, my wife, and I walked into the office, held hands together, and prayed. We all trembled. My wife and I walked to our bedroom where I fetched a short pair of trousers, a toothbrush, toothpaste, *Faith for Daily Living* (a spiritual tract), and a Bible. "We do not accept Bibles," said the captain as he gave the Bible back to my wife. I kissed my two young daughters and Reggy and started out.

"Shall we ever see each other again, darling?" asked Reggy anxiously.

"I do not know. If I die, praise the Lord; if I live, praise the Lord."

I walked ahead, they behind. My wife, mother, and eldest sister followed me to the car. As we drove away I could hear my mother's faint voice in the distance: "My son again! My only son! Oh, God! You police, why don't you drive over me rather than cause me all these heartaches? Now is the third time . . ."

At Palmaryville we had a flat tire. I opened the door to help but was pushed back. "Stay inside." When we passed the Presidential Palace the captain burst into a series of accusations: "Why do you want to over-throw the government? Why do you preach nonsense? Why. . . ? Why. . . ? Why. . . ? You think we shall play with you?"

At the Sibasa security-police building, I was forced to sit on the steps in a room with pictures of weapons of all sorts displayed on the wall, a horrible sight. The police hurriedly ate their porridge and meat, locked me behind in a van, and drove north at top speed. At the sharp curves my head banged against the sides of the van. We passed Venda Central Prison. At the junction to Donald Fraser Hospital the van dropped one of its headlights. We ended up at Masisi police station, near the Zim-babwe border. I was searched. My *Faith for Daily Living* tract was con-fiscated by a member of my congregation, one who on several occasions sang the liturgy before I preached, an elder of our Lutheran church. He instructed the warrant officer to make life very difficult for me and threatened stern measures if the instructions were not heeded. I was also instructed to get pen and paper from the station commander to prepare a statement since, as the security police sergeant put it, "You know your crimes."

Masisi is a small holding police station with four cells, two for women and two for men. The roofs and the walls are corrugated iron, the floor concrete. There are water toilets in the cells, and before the cells, sur-rounded by a security fence, one shower cubicle also of corrugated iron, in each section. This is one of the hottest parts of South Africa, ranging between thirty-five and forty-two degrees Celsius in summer. And it was summer. It felt like being in an oven. I was locked up in one of the cells in the women's section.

The food was horrible, to say the least. I protested to no avail. Mostly I lived on grace rather than food. Human beings can be very cruel to one another. They can become beasts. Usually, uniformed policemen treated the prisoners well. But there were scattered instances of torture. The only policewoman was very rude in her dealings with prisoners. Jy sal kak jong, jou kak jong! ("You will excrete, you excrement!"), she would say, and many other unprintable words flowed out of her like the Zambezi river. When she was off duty, she would come back and taunt the male prisoners verbally and by her manners. It was some kind of game to her.

Interrogation

On November 23, three security policemen came, a captain, a ser-geant, and a policewoman, quite young. I had previously complained of pain at the back of my head caused by the banging in the police van. I was interrogated in the station commander's office, always standing. I was accused of having been in contact with lawyers in Johannesburg to seek legal aid for the family of Ike Muofhe, of having made plans for evil to occur against the police either before or during or after Ike's funeral. The police also wanted to know what I would have preached at the funeral had they not detained me. In addition, they accused me of participating in the attack on the police station. A few minutes later, they produced a "terrorist" who claimed to have been with me during the attack. It was totally unbelievable. In faltering Venda, the "terrorist" said, "Do not speak nonsense. You know me. We were together. Do not play. Do not fool yourself. You got me into trouble." I was totally dumbfounded. Did the police not know for sure where I had been on the night in question? The captain threatened me: "You have been in detention before. If you do not cooperate we shall do to you the kak which the Afrikaners did to you. I will crush your testicles before this lady. Make up your mind; we will be back on the twenty-fifth with sophisticated torture equipment." That left me trembling. In my cell, I fell on my knees and called upon my God of Pietermaritzburg, of Sibasa, of Louis Trichardt, and of Pietersburg. The Lord revealed to me that tougher days lay ahead. To make matters worse, I did not even have a Bible except for the one that the police could not confiscate, in my memory.

They arrived on the twenty-fifth, as promised. I was subjected to a day-long interrogation and accusations, always standing except for the lunch hour, when they shared their meal with me, porridge and very good fat beef, rather oversalted. At the end they were very angry with my statement, since, they claimed, it was not a confession. "We are tired of you. You are always attacking apartheid. You ridicule Vendaland. You want the whole of South Africa . . . no, the whole of Africa. We shall eradicate you. You will never see your so-called freedom, neither will your children, nor perhaps your grandchildren. You want the white man's towns, cities, and industries. Why don't you develop your own? Come on, write farewell letters to your wife, your bishop, friends, and relatives. Tell them you have escaped from prison across the border to Mozambique. The letters must be ready tomorrow. We have no choice. We have to kill you and throw your body into Mozambique. They will say you have been killed by your communist brothers. We need the letters to exonerate ourselves." At the end of his lecture, the captain handed me sheets of paper and a pen. I accepted and agreed to write. I was dead scared. But before he locked me up, I called out, "Take your things. I will not write." He was furious. "If you write, that is better for you. For we shall kill you quickly and it will be all over. If you do not, we shall torture you very slowly, and you will die a very painful death." I still refused to write. It was not that I was brave. They left me in unspeakable fear.

The Lord No Comfort to the Uncomfortable

I prayed. I fasted. I confessed my sins. The Lord absolved me. I prayed. I fasted. I meditated. Day in and day out. At times for three days. At times for four. Even five. Before Christmas I landed in Donald Fraser Hospital twice. The doctor was very kind. I could not share everything with him. Under these circumstances, whom can one trust? I saw him on December 18 and on the twenty-first. He instructed the police to bring me for further examination on the sixth of January, 1982. It was not to be.

I enjoyed Christmas day. It was the first real Christmas in my life. I do not mean food, clothes, or drinks but the real birth of Christ.

In several visions the Lord revealed to me that I would be terribly tortured and subjected to electrical shock. The visions were so real that several nights I moved to the center of the cell fearing that the security police might electrocute me through the corrugated iron walls. God, I felt, was very unkind to me.

If You Live, We Do Not Know Our Job

They came on January 4, in the morning. There were at least three of them: the captain, the sergeant, and one whose rank was kept secret. Perhaps he was unranked. From the outset they were uncompromising. I was forced to sit on an imaginary chair, then to rest on my clenched fists on the floor, with my legs stretched backwards. I was forced to stand on my head, my legs raised, pushed against the wall. In this position I received kicks from all angles. I was forced to lie on my back, raise my legs, and open them. The captain kicked my genitals. I rolled in pain, excruciating pain. "I am determined," he said, "to destroy your manhood, those dirty testicles that make you feel like a small bull." They threw me into the air and let me fall on the concrete floor several times. They lifted me into the air by my hair. They pulled off my beard and hair. They banged my head against the wall, hit me with sticks and chairs. Punches landed on my head, stomach, chest, ears, everywhere. It was a total onslaught. Karate chops and judo kicks took their toll. During this nightmarish experience I bled profusely and lost consciousness several times.

Toward evening, I was forced to clean the blood on the floor and to use the same cloth to wipe the blood on my body and face. I was badly injured and swollen. My head was swollen, my nose and mouth bleeding, my eyes so swollen and bloodied I could hardly see. I was bleeding and breathing through the ears: my ear drums were punctured. The wounds on the knees were so deep I could put in the tips of my fingers.

They dragged me from the torture room. I was thrown into a pickup truck, handcuffed to the bars, and covered with a blanket. "If you are alive by tomorrow morning," shouted the captain self-assuredly, "then we do not know our job." He added, "If you uncover yourself on the way, *jy sal kak*." We drove away at top speed. Somewhere along the way he stopped and dropped off one of his colleagues. "Goodbye, Brother Rams. We'll see each other tomorrow."

They threw me into a very dirty, muddy, smelly cell at Sibasa police station[6] and told me to be ready to meet Brother Joe the following day. I thought it was a human being. I was wrong. In the center of that cell, I looked like a mound of pain, a severed piece of elephant flesh.

The morning was not long in coming. Two of them fetched me in a new white car. It was driven by my liturgically minded parishioner. We headed for the security police building at Sibasa, opposite Lukoto Bus Depot, a mere seven kilometers from my home, wife, mother, and children.

"No man enters this room and goes out alive unless he says and does what we want," said the tall sergeant as they moved me into a room, closed the door and then the curtains. I was forced to undress. Only my underpants remained on my body. They put a canvas bag over my head. Water was poured on the floor. A gluelike substance was poured over my spinal cord. Electric wires were connected to my earlobes and back of the neck. After pouring water over my head, they switched on the current. I jerked and collapsed into the water, the electric wires still on. From morning till noon I went through this process. I cried like a baby and begged for mercy. In response the police sang, led by their dedicated captain, "Hallelujah, let us praise the Lord." The overzealous captain mocked me: "Dean, you are a man of God. Call God! He will help you!"

---

[6]The drive from Masisi to Sibasa is about 100 km.

I prayed to God, "Please take my life. I cannot take it any longer." Whenever I would lose consciousness, I accepted this as God's answer to my prayer request, only to be disappointed when I regained consciousness. They gave me about fifteen minutes of rest while they had their lunch and I sat in the water, handcuffed behind my back. The handcuffs literally bit into my flesh. I pleaded, to no avail. I was hungry and very thirsty. For two days I had had nothing for food and drink except the water I managed to gulp when they poured it over my head.

After lunch, I would not have my head covered. There was a long struggle. They kicked, punched, kneed my groin, and eventually I succumbed as I fell into the water. "He wants to be martyr. A second martyr. We shall extract all the communism out of his head. If he wants to experience all our advanced methods he shall have them," said my faithful parishioner. They connected electric wires to my toes, thighs, and only then did I discover that the undershorts were left on the body not out of respect but as a fertile ground for planting electric wires through the opening. "We will see how he will perform on his wife if he is lucky enough to leave this room alive," declared the captain. They turned on the electricity. My whole body shook, my insides danced. It was the most excruciating pain of my life. I wondered if it could be worse in hell. They brought in young boys to look at my nakedness and laugh at me. They did an expert job. Perhaps that was part of their training? The white colonel in charge opened the door, looked at me, and laughed: "I had never expected to see the dean in this position." There were other white faces I could not recognize; they deliberately kept out of view. I caught only glimpses of them.

As I sat in the water, half dead, half alive, the senior, stouter captain sat on the table and gave me a long lecture: "Dean, you think you are clever. You are a fool. Do you remember your sermons? [He listed a number of places and dates.] You are actually a dog. We only gave you a long rope so you could hang yourself. You . . . you . . ." The ever-silent sergeant said coolly from behind his sunglasses, "If you ever become president of this country we would rather leave the country than live under your government." A conglomeration of mockings and allegations then flew at me from all angles. "Who bought your car? Your furniture? How much money do you get from the organization? You are a little boy; who is younger than you among us? We shall not stop torturing you until you add your urine to your blood and mix it with water. Clever Farisani! You are misled by overseas churches. They use money to buy you and have you oppose the government. People would even like you to be a bishop here in Vendaland. How much money do you earn per month?

That is too little. There is somebody who holds an important position in the government which was supposed to be yours. [They mentioned his name.] Twenty-five hundred rand per month! Or you can be archbishop of all the churches in Venda. That's three thousand rand! Your pastors can earn a lot of money. Five hundred rand?! Where do you get the money to pay for your trips to Johannesburg, Pietersburg, and many other places? Who pays you? Which organization? Which weapons were used during the attack on the police station? AK 47s? Rockets? Hand grenades? The terrorists fled back to Johannesburg? How? Which road did they follow? Of course they hid their weapons. Where? There was a meeting before the attack. Where? And . . . and . . . and . . . and . . ."

I was baffled. I decided to respond only to one important question, just to tell the truth before I died. "I do not aspire to be a bishop. I have never so aspired. To me a bishop who does not do his work honestly is no better than an ordinary evangelist, deaconess, pastor, or dean. What counts in God's work is not the status but dedication, devotion, and faith. I do not want to be a bishop." This did not come out of bravery but came out of the conviction that I would die any minute.

Someone, probably a lieutenant colonel, gave me papers and a pen and charged me to describe the preparation of the attack, the boys who visited me, the boys who visited my friend, Pastor Phosiwa, how the police station was attacked, what kind of weapons were used, where the vehicles were parked, how the guerrillas left, where they hid their weapons.

The captain ordered one of the security police to prepare boiling water to pour up my . . . My Christian brothers and sisters, my God, please forgive me. I could not take more torture. I heard the kettle boiling. I realized the seriousness of the statement "No one comes into this room and goes out alive unless he says and does what we want." I did agree to write in the cell. "Yes, Dean, write peacefully, you are not under duress," emphasized the lieutenant colonel.

I was allowed to dress. My short pair of trousers, my undershirt, black sweater, and sandals. All were dirty and partly wet from two days of hard labor. I was driven back to Sibasa police station and dumped into my cell.

Take My Life

That evening I offered my life to God: "God, do me one favor. Take my life before I betray your integrity, your truth, and your way, before I write a lot of lies. I have tried always to be a man of truth and of principle. I cannot any longer. Do your job tonight. You heard the lieutenant colonel putting the suggestion of suicide to me: 'Dean Farisani, do not commit suicide. We know you will not. You have a strong will.' " Earlier that evening, and also the night before, they had locked me in the cell without removing my belt as the regulations require. I said to God then and to myself, "I will never do their dirty job for them, even if it means more electric shocks." I collapsed into a deep sleep, hoping to die. Pretoria seemed to be looking from above, saying, "Here lies communism and subversion, suffocated by the poisonous gas of unpatriotism. Let all such never rest until they are in bloody pieces."

Imagine my frustration when the next morning, January 6, Mother Consciousness carried me in her cold, bony arms into the world of the living. I was not dead, just a swollen heap of flesh. The bread and milk brought into the cell the night before by my faithful security police liturgist still lay intact. It seemed to look at my empty stomach in confused amazement. But how *could* I eat? For what purpose? Do we not eat to live? Do we ever eat to die?

Transgression of Their First Commandment

I did not write the statement. I could not. Half-blind bloodied eyes, heavy swollen arms and fingers, open wounds on wrists and knee caps, waves of pain from the center of the brain to the toe tips, lifeless genitals reduced to one-fourth in size—there, on the concrete floor, lay a mound of human flesh, drowned in despair and pain. In the evening I burst out, "God, tonight please. Do not delay. They are coming for their confession." That night, light, or rather lightning, flashed into my cell: "My son do not despair, I shall save your life." I collapsed into the deep waters of undisturbed sleep on the comfortable mattress of this promise.

Their Will Is Done

On the seventh I was still alive. I knew they would come, so I started to scribble. I wrote and wrote, and wrote: One car was parked under a big tree; another stopped near the shop. A car with Johannesburg plates was parked near the hotel, full of Azapo members, with AK 47s, hand grenades. After the attack on the police station, the weapons were hidden in the bushes near our water engine . . . and this, and that. Also that. Even that. What a mixture! May I be saved from reading this nonsense today, and from even finding myself in another situation like that.

Blasphemy and Adoration

Then the almighty lieutenant colonel came. The statement was not ready, not waiting for him. After sending his junior on what appeared to be an empty errand, he whispered, "We know, we are convinced, that you committed no crime. We know you are innocent. But the other people—the other pastors . . . I am so sorry that all our good pastors may die . . . but just write. Just write what you confessed the other day. Just write." When two (or three) security policemen came in the afternoon, my outrageous confession was already completed in black and white—ready-made death-row material for my friends and myself. They handcuffed me, this time in front, not behind my back. In the van, seated in front between them, I started cursing within myself: God, you lied to me. You promised to save my life. Now they are taking me to a more sophisticated torture station. They have found out that my 'confession' is a heap of rotten nonsense. Why did you command me not to despair? You are betraying me."

When the van turned right, into Tshilidzini hospital on the afternoon of January 7, 1982, I recanted my blasphemies with double the speed I made them: "Oh, forgive my blasphemies, Lord. I am a liar, not you. I am a traitor, not you. I am unreliable and unstable, not you. I am a sinner, but you are good. Pardon me, forgive me, Lord. Truly you shall save my life."

In dirty, muddy sandals, dirty, smelling underpants, and a short pair of trousers, a white undershirt turned brown, and a sweat-clotted sweater, black but shining with body oil spotted with blood, and having my hair uncombed, like tufts of grass with clean patches in between, thanks to the unskillful shaving and hair-cutting methods of the police, I marched between them, the open wounds clearly visible to all who cared to see. And many hospital visitors did see, among them a young student who, because he seemed to care more than was officially permissible, was himself detained for seven months immediately thereafter.

"Remove the handcuffs," the senior doctor demanded. They did, reluctantly. Two more doctors came, perhaps to act as witnesses. In a whisper the senior doctor asked, "Are you Dean Farisani?"

"Yes."

"The police have hurt you."

A thorough check up followed. As I walked to the X-ray section, I looked into many known faces, among them members of my circuit. Some took off their hats, others saluted, a few nodded. Several closed their eyes, and a number looked away. One old lady, standing against the wall in the passage, looked straight into heaven. I looked ahead, while the police looked straight into their sunglasses. The policemen refused to stand outside during either the doctor's or the X-ray man's examination. Even medical institutions and personnel are compelled to say, "Let thy will be done as in Pretoria, so also in this hospital." There may be exceptions, but they are very few.

"Do not look sideways," the police mumbled as they led me back to the police van, again handcuffed but stocked with ointments, medicines, and pills.

I was thrown into my dirty, muddied cell, medicines and all—to be my own doctor and nurse. I decided not to use the medicines. What for? A kind-hearted policeman came and put the ointments in my eyes, ears, and nose, and anointed my wounds. The dirty shower was made available to me. I did not use it. I could not. In fact why should I? To what end? At least in these areas, my will, not Pretoria's, would be done.

Suspicious Comfort

The next day, January 8, I was admitted to the same hospital. I must admit I was shocked and surprised. In my secluded ward, guarded by armed policemen who worked in relays of eight hours, I lay in a comfortable bed in a suspiciously comfortable atmosphere. Many of the nurses were kind and friendly; so were the doctors and the uniformed police (these are not security police). One nurse openly hated me, however. Another, who had already found me guilty, was more subtle, but her eyes and movements betrayed her true self.

The meals were good, very good. They were too good to be true. But did I enjoy it? What was it for? To what end? After all, was I not being fattened for slaughter, for another electrocution dose?

I am not used to being bathed by women, even if they are nurses. So I asked the police to help me bathe. Friendly uniformed policemen did help to bathe me, and we had not just cold but also hot water. Perhaps it is true that Lucifer was an angel before he turned into a devil. Something angelic still remains in him. From somewhere in a sacred corner of the hospital, some Christian music drifted faintly into my room:

> Halelujah we have shamed the devil,
> Let us tread upon him,
> Halelujah we have shamed the devil.

For the next few days in hospital, this refrain helped to keep my bearings clear—spiritually and mentally. It was like the wings of a large eagle that carried me above my earlier horrible experiences and my present pains.

The security police came on January 13. I said goodbye to those friendly nurses and uniformed police, to the uplifting music, the flower of hope at one corner of the room, the green grass and the large tree outside. I said goodbye to the mortuary nearby that stood at the ready should the will of Pretoria be done. Loaded with pills, ointments, and cotton to stuff in my damaged ears, I followed the angels of death out of hospital while the powerless, loving hospital staff and visitors looked on. Pretoria! Thy will be done!

Back to the Jungle Oven Cell

That day, I was allowed to collect my personal belongings from my muddied cell at Sibasa, now already occupied by the lonely young student who had dared look at me. His face was swollen, his hair and beard pulled out. We exchanged glances, a dangerous, criminal act in detention. I left that cell, carrying the one smelly blanket that was used to cover me after my ordeal at Masisi on January 4.

They took me back to my familiar corrugated-iron cell at Masisi, which by this time I had grown to love and kept spotlessly clean. I was allowed some freedom to go outside the cell and into the courtyard, which was surrounded by high security fences. During the day I was practically unhindered from using the corrugated cubicle shower. I nursed my own wounds, kneecaps, wrists, and put cotton wool into my ears to prevent water infection. The pains in my legs and at the back of my neck were still unbearable. I became my own doctor. The police kept the medicines but brought them to me at regular intervals, three times a day.

It was hot, very hot. The wounds were now closing up, though the pains were still severe. I fasted and prayed day and night. I used to sing, moving in circles both in the cell and the courtyard:

> I will walk tall, I will walk tall,
> I will walk tall in Jesus' name!
> Food with worms, I will eat tall,
> I will eat tall in Jesus' name,
> Blankets smelling, I will sleep tall in Jesus' name,
> I will sleep tall in Jesus' name.
> Wounds all over, I will walk tall in Jesus' name,
> I will walk tall in Jesus' name.
> My wife away, Reggy away,
> I will walk tall in Jesus' name.

> My children away, Ndzumbu away, Ndamu away,
> I will walk tall in Jesus' name.
> Congregations away, I will walk tall in Jesus' name!
> Pangs of prison, I walk tall in Jesus' name!
> Pains of jail, I walk tall in Jesus' name!
> Tall fences around, I walk taller in Jesus' name!

During periods of depression I would argue with God in song, in my mother tongue:

Fhumula Tshenu	Be calm, Tshenu
Fhumula Tshenu	Be calm, Tshenu
Fhumula nwana wanga	Be calm, my child
Thi fhumuli baba	I will not keep quiet, Father
Thi fhumuli Mune wanga	I will not keep quiet, Lord
Mbonzhe ngedzi	Here are my wounds
Vhutungu ngovhu	The searing pain
Zwi khou vhavha Mune wanga	It is painful, Lord
Fhumula Tshenu	Be calm, Tshenu
Ndi khou zwi vhona nwana wanga	I see that, my child
Mutshidzi ndi nne nwana wanga	I am the savior, my child
Ndo zwi pfa baba	I understand, Father
Ndo tenda baba	I believe, Father
Ndikhou edela Mune wanga	I am now sleeping, Lord
Ho fara iwe khotsi anga.	Now lead me on, Father.

I sang often these and many other songs, not always the same words and not always in the same sequence. In the evenings I sang, first standing, then sitting, and finally lying on my mat, often singing myself into sleep.

They Watch and Wonder

The uniformed police saw me before I was tortured, and they saw me on January 4, after the first torture. They saw me again on the thirteenth, and after February 5. They saw my health, and my wounds. They watched as I lost more weight daily. One day, one of the uniformed policemen at Masisi asked, "Dean, who is your God?"

"Jehovah."

"Is he greater than our ancestors?"

"Yes."

"Is your God the one who rescued Israel from Egypt?"

"Yes."

"Why does he not help you then?" He dried his tears with the back of his muscular hand. "This God," he mumbled, "is on the side of whites. He does not care for you—for any of us. Look, you are—we are all—

suffering. We work for them. We make money for them. We kill one another for them. We cannot beat them. They have everything; they can *do* anything. Pretoria is everything . . . these buildings, these uniforms, these handcuffs, the vans, the petrol. We *must* obey them. They are our god. We must serve them. What else can we do? But you believe God will help you."

The Flesh Is Weak, the
Spirit Is Strong

On the first day of February I received a parcel of clothes and toiletries from Regina, that loving and brave woman whom God has given to me. I was a very happy man, a very important prisoner (VIP) in the clean, perfumed clothes.

That afternoon witnessed a very different story. I became very sick. I was taken to Madimbo Army Base, where the military doctor listened to the story of my torture with learned disinterest. He instructed the military nurse to inject me in each buttock, then gave me large pills and a gargle lotion. "If a pastor is only concerned with God's Word, how can he be detained?" he said.

February 2 found me growing weaker and weaker. I walked into the shower cubicle but felt dizzy. I came out and tried to hold on to the fence and then collapsed. I gave one last scream. Heavy heart palpitations. Then no heart beat. My body was cold, very cold. I could not move a finger. I felt very thirsty. A kind police sergeant managed to get water down the throat every minute or two. I could hardly speak. The body would be very cold and then very hot.

On the way to Madimbo Army Base, I drifted between reality and unreality, between consciousness and unconsciousness: "Bye-bye Reggy, bye-bye Ndzumbu and Ndamu, bye-bye Mummy and Daddy, bye-bye congregations, bye-bye trees, good-bye life. God will look after you. Thank you God. Now I am going to rest, free at last from torture and harassment." I joined the choir that had started singing in very melodious voices: "What a friend we have in Jesus . . ."

At Madimbo the doctor looked into the van, felt my pulse, gave me a blue pill and water, saying, "Is this the man who was here yesterday? I am not supposed to treat patients from Venda. [Did he know that the supervisors and engineers of my torture were not Venda, but whites?] Drive him to the nearest hospital. He may—he will make it. If he dies in my hands I will have to answer many questions."

Back at Masisi, I asked the police to take along my Madimbo medicines. They drove me, lying in the back of a van, 120 kilometers to Tshilidzini hospital. That evening, the second, I was admitted, only to be removed on February 5 to the Sibasa torture station. In the familiar torture room, I was coached on how to make my "confession" to a magistrate. I was then moved to the lieutenant colonel's office, where he read a typed statement to me. I objected to many falsifications of my already-false statement, which the colonel ascribed to typing errors. When I objected that the very core of the statement was false, he threatened to begin at square one, and I immediately succumbed and signed the false statement, which actually deviated from my nonsensical "confession." After this I was given coffee to drink. Or was it tea?

We went to Tshandama, the magistrate office, which is forty kilometers away. My torturers sat outside, next to the door, within hearing distance of all that was said.

"To whom will you give my statement after this?"

"Back to the police," said the tall magistrate, in the presence of his interpreter. (The discussions were in English, although we were all blacks.)

"Are you doing this voluntarily?" he asked.

I could hear the heavy breathing of the torturers at the entrance. This magistrate had himself been a police officer a few years before. "If you are giving this statement to them," I said, "I shall repeat what I have already told them. Look at my wrists, my kneecaps, my eyes, the side of my head, my testicles. I do not want to suffer any more."

"Now would you describe what you see, interpreter?" the magistrate asked.

"A scar, two scars, laceration, laceration, dry wounds," said the interpreter. "They are not old," he added.

Having noted this, the magistrate looked at me: "And now, your statement?"

"I have no choice. I do not want to be harmed again." And I repeated it, the colonel's story, with explanations, as instructed.

Back at Sibasa, my statement was read by the senior security police. In the interim, a young security police boy, a teenager, came and sat beside me in the car. "What do you study at the Lutheran Theological College? What subjects? Where do you get these communistic ideas from—from Germany, Europe, and America? From East Germany? Some of your teachers must come from East Germany and infiltrate the church. Do you pray? Does your God answer you? Don't waste your time. It is already too late. You are in big trouble. OK, if you want, you may pray."

I exploded for the first time in a long time. "What do you know about theology? About God? I do not pray to you, I pray to God. You do not answer my prayers, God does. I shall continue to serve and pray to the Lord, whether you believe in prayer or not."

"You are becoming cheeky again?" He left the car and went to the seniors. At any time hell could break loose. Probably the devil was on leave: nothing happened.

Again, into the van they led me. That night I slept at Tshandama police station. The whole weekend the words of the bespectacled security sergeant at Sibasa kept ringing in my head: "We shall come and fetch you tomorrow, Sunday, or Monday." They fetched me on Monday, February 8, to the torture room, then to the colonel's office, and then to the room of Captain White, formerly Sergeant White. "How are you, Dean?" he asked.

"I am not feeling well. Since I left hospital I am feeling very weak."

"Were you in hospital? What happened? I did not know that!"

I pressed my lips, and said loudly within myself, "You are a murderous liar."

The Innocent Criminal

"Where are you leading me?" I asked.

"To court," the sergeant retorted.

"What crime have I committed?"

"You know. You heard something and kept quiet."

"Am I an informer, to inform you about your own traps? I am innocent; I am not guilty of any crime."

We stopped at the entrance. Inside the court was in session. It was 3:30 in the afternoon of February 8. I was hurried back to the car without explanation.

Back in the car, I looked at the van parked behind us. In the locked van sat R. T., a young man vehemently opposed to corruption and apartheid. He was thin, haggard, and dazed. More police cars parked around mine. Detainees filed into the courtroom. I opened my door to join them but was stopped by Colonel White: "You are not going. I will see you, not today but at a later stage. Take him to Venda Central Prison, chaps." That evening I found myself seventeen kilometers away in a small cell, only three cells from the one in which Isaac Muofhe had been found dead on the toilet almost three months before. I was told this immediately by the other detainees.

I loved this prison, for the fellowship of the other detainees, in spite of the dividing walls; for the music of the convicts and those awaiting trial. I loved the comparatively good food, the regular showers and exercise— at times, in groups of two, three, or even four. I loved the medical attention and the police nurses, though during my stay no doctor came. I loved our common prayers, sermons, Bible studies, fasting, topical discussions, singing, sharing of sorrows and joys and dreams. I loved the cleaning of our cells and passage, and visits by some friendly uniformed police.

I hated this prison. I hated the small toilet and washbasin, the iron grilles at the door, always too stubborn to let one's head out. I hated visits by security police at night, which often led to the removal of one of us for nocturnal interrogation. I hated listening to the stories of the "graduates," those from the torture chamber. I hated the insults by some uniformed policemen.

"Dean Farisani, why are you here?"

"Because I wanted to overthrow the government, because I am a terrorist, a communist, and a subversive." I had discovered this is the only language they understand, the only pepper they swallow without flinching, the only honey that burns their arrogant lips like hot chili. I hated the hypocritical sloganeering, twice, thrice a day: "Any complaint? Problems? Worries?" Almost always, this Good Samaritan asked the question with his mouth open as wide as his ears were tightly closed. Lodging complaints was often regarded as a healthy ventilation of detainees' pent-up emotions. I hated all the good things, because nothing is good in detaining innocent people. I hate detention and torture and murder . . . lonely moments, no sun, no trees, no newspapers, no wife, no children, no friends, no Bible, no books, no truth, no control, no decency, no limits, no life, no freedom. A kingdom of brutal beasts, of spineless ghosts that unleash their lunacy on helpless victims hooded and handcuffed at the back. A kingdom whose statue of liberty is the violation of human rights. Here Pretoria's will is done.

Hospital, Hope, and Hugs

On February 19, I reached for the emergency call button in the cell but collapsed halfway. I screamed once and no more. My detainee neighbor had heard the scream and the thud, and alerted the other detainees. All of them pressed their emergency call buttons. It was about eight in the morning. I turned, rolled, and wriggled. This was the second heart attack, if we ignore some minor heart trouble at Tshandama. "Water, fresh air, water, fresh air, water, fresh air," I pleaded.

"Give him water, Sergeant, but do not take him out of the cell. There's enough fresh air in the cell. The door is open. We have no authority. We shall have to get permission. You know them, you know them."

I tried to reach for the water jug, but in vain. Breathlessness . . . general weakness . . . I had a desire to die. Nine. Ten. Eleven. Twelve o'clock.

"What is wrong Dean?" asked the liturgist of torture.

"Water, fresh air, water, fresh air," I heaved.

One, two, three, four. At four-thirty I was again in Tshilidzini hospital. Once I was in the doctor's hands, the liturgist left. I looked around; not a single policeman was present. The nurses wheeled me to the emergency ward, where I lay next to another very ill man, legs raised in traction. An hour or two later, an armed uniformed policeman arrived.

The next morning, on February 20, I was transferred to my familiar secluded ward, conveniently situated next to the mortuary, from where I could watch, day and night, as new inmates were carted into the kingdom of the silent. I was very sick. During my early days in the hospital the Venda attorney general came to ask about my statement to the police. I asked him whether he had seen the one I had made during the questioning at Masisi in November. He said he had not. I told him that that was the only truthful statement I had made, that the other was the product of the wounds he could see on my body. Did he need a true statement? I asked for stationery and wrote as best I could a copy of the only true statement, the one the police had rejected on November 25.

The turn of events started with the arrival of Deputy Bishop Uwe Hollm, from Berlin. He took my hand, smiled broadly, and assured me of God's love and care. I told him I wanted to see my family, or at least my family photo. We prayed, and he left.

Sometime in March, my wife and daughters came. Reggy and I looked at each other, neither of us believing what we saw. We embraced and kissed, and for a moment disappeared into the world of unreality. Ndzumbu, my first daughter, climbed onto my bed, making certain not to come too close to the stranger on the other side. "This is Daddy, this is Mummy, this is Granny, this is Ndamu [the younger sister], and this is Ndzumbu [herself]," she said as she skillfully moved her little finger from one figure to another on the photo that I had posted on the wall.

"Here is your father, Ndzumbu. Kiss him!" My wife picked her up and brought her to me. She resisted. "No, this is not my father; my father is the one in the photo." Tears welled up in my wife's eyes—and mine. I had lost thirty kilograms (about sixty-five pounds). My wife later explained, "You had changed; you were completely different. You were not the one I knew. I cannot explain it. You had changed: your eyes—you were swollen—your head, your arms. You were different. I do not know..."

A visit from the team of the International Red Cross from overseas was unexpected but reassuring. The police refused to leave and stood behind the short partition behind my bed. I showed them the marks of torture and told them the story in faltering German. They asked whether they should go to the government with my story; I answered affirmatively. They reassured me that they would try to do their best so that I would not suffer the same things in the future.

Then came a white magistrate, who identified himself as Mr. K. He was the first magistrate to visit me since December 18. Between then and now no magistrate had dared visit me, lest Pretoria's will be undone. "I am visiting you as the law requires that I visit all state witnesses," he declared. "How are you?"

"I am what you see," I said, showing him the marks of torture on my knees, wrists, and side of the head, and I added, "If you so wish, I can show you marks on my genitals."

Confounded, he said, "I am not coming for that today. I will see you again."

"But sir," I said, "has the criminal investigating officer not told you that I am bringing criminal charges against the security police for torture? Are you not aware that my statement is already with the attorney general? How do you say that I am a state witness? You gave me a paper; nobody ever discussed this with me. It is not right; it is not fair!"

He left.

This was really baffling. Had I not told the attorney general that my first true statement had never reached him, that the one in his office was a product of duress and torture? Had I not then written another one from my hospital bed?

After this Colonel White visited me in hospital. "We want to advise you to withdraw your charges against the police. No man can fight against the government and win. Do you want the police to go to prison?"

"Are the police and the government identical?" I wondered within myself. "The logic is clear: Whoever opposes the police opposes the government. Whoever opposes the government opposes the police."

"Withdraw your charges. We are also withdrawing our charges against you," Colonel White instructed.

"But I have not been charged. I have committed no crime," I responded.

"I mean . . . I mean . . . you must withdraw your charges!" he insisted. I was dead scared. I asked for time to think about it.

When the attorney general came once more, I asked whether I was really protected from possible further torture. "As long as you are here, they cannot torture you," he replied, "but if they remove you, we cannot guarantee anything." I got the message. When the other colonel and again Colonel White came, I agreed to suspend the charges till further notice. Colonel White dictated the letter, including the part that read, "I am doing this voluntarily and not under duress of any sort," or something like that. I signed it, and Colonel White bade me farewell, carrying his precious booty. "Our father who art in Pretoria . . . thy kingdom has come . . . thy will is done . . . at gunpoint . . . even in hospital . . . the wronged are forced to cooperate with thee."

In the meantime Pastor A. Mahamba had joined me in the ward. This time we were allowed to read books, have tape recorders and cassettes for music, and were allowed visits by our families once a week. We were also visited by church leaders. Among others, Professor and Mrs. K. Nürnberger, Deans P. M. Masekela and M. C. Mminele, who celebrated Holy Communion with us, Dr. A. Van Niekerk, Bishop Martin Kruse, and Herbert Meissner all came to visit.

My mother, poor mother, visited me regularly, eyes full of despair, heart full of hope.

The University of South Africa got permission from the attorney general for me to write my examinations, which I had missed in January and February, on April 26 and 29.

On June 1, after a court case against my good friends Pastors Phaswana and Phosiwa had ended, I was driven to the Supreme Court by the security police and told that I was released. Many people were waiting for me, among them my dear wife. She accompanied me as I was led into an office where I was given a form to claim almost four hundred rand for the days I spent in prison as a "potential state witness." I never claimed this blood money.

I was then led to Colonel White, who gave me an ointment for the pains in my legs. I was in the company of my wife and attorney. "This is a very good ointment. My brother [or was it brother-in-law?] uses it on his cattle, but on himself too. It works perfectly well." I dedicated that ointment to the evil ones who torture and murder, and left it as a souvenir to a free South Africa. We drove back to the hospital, and got permission to attend the thanksgiving service led by West Berlin's Bishop

Kruse. After the service we drove back to hospital, where the doctor, with tears in his eyes, discharged me and asked me to return to the hospital regularly for treatment. When I walked out of the ward I bumped into a group of nurses, just emerging from prayers for our release. I told them I had been released. They screamed in joy and excitement, some fell to the floor, others clung to me, a few others wept. We drove home.

Home

I was very weak and overweight. Six meals a day in hospital had raised my sixty-five kilograms to a staggering 105, a terrible thing for a five-foot, six-inch individual. That night we enjoyed our normal family evening. The powerful captain's kicks had not succeeded.

The next morning my eldest daughter knocked on the bedroom door and inquired, "Is Daddy in the room?" When I said, "Yes, Ndzumbu, I am here. Come in," she ran away in unbelievable joy, only to come back and say, "Will the police take you again? Did they beat you, Daddy? Did you cry? Do you love them? Are the police the children of God? Is Isaac Muofhe dead? Will he ever come back again? Did the police take you to the clouds?" How I wished that Pretoria could be forced to answer all these questions.

On the afternoon of June 3 Colonel White arrived at my home. "Here are your exam results. Open, let us see!" The letter was dated about May 19. I opened it. "Very good. You have done very well. Excellent. Unbelievable." I thanked God for this miracle, and deep down in my heart I said, "You have shamed the devil, you have trodden upon his head, your name be praised."

"And now, will you please write on this paper to withdraw your charges against the police," Colonel White asked—demanded.

"Give me time, Colonel, give me time," I said.

I discussed the problem with my bishop, then with my lawyer. We all concluded that my chances of surviving through a trial against the police were nil. I handed the "claim form for state-witness fees" to my lawyer and instructed him to withdraw the criminal charges lest they withdraw my life from me. Later Pastors Phaswana, Phosiwa, and I did bring civil damage suits against the police.

On June 13 my daughter and my wife's niece were baptized. The names we had given our daughter shouted a relevant message: "Ndamulelo ["redemption"] Mbofholowo ["freedom"] Farisani, I baptize you in the name of the Father, Son, and the Holy Spirit. . . ."

NO TO
APARTHEID

Telling the Truth

Between October 19, 1982, and February 11, 1983, I told the stories of my torture both in Europe and in the United States of America, to individuals, Amnesty International groups, organizations, congregations, parishes, synods, mayors, government officials, and advisers. I thanked them all for what they had done to speak and act for my release.

A few days after my return from abroad I was picked up by three security police, two of whom were actually involved in my torture and against whom I was pressing damage claims. On arrival at their headquarters, I was received by the cruelest security police captain—the one who led and participated in my torture. Was it legal and acceptable that my torturers be again my prosecutors and judges? In South Africa, we are in trouble, big trouble.

My interrogation was conducted by two senior policemen, one of whom participated in helping supervise my previous torture. I was threatened with a banning order if I could not learn to discipline my mouth on international platforms. "No government can afford to allow its police to be exposed in this fashion!" Of course, the question arises, would not a government that truly has any respect for justice and human rights rather honor me with a medal for exposing these terrible, terroristic violations of human rights? Would it not appoint an independent commission of inquiry into detention without trial, torture and death in detention? Would it not prosecute the offenders and abolish all the laws that are fertile ground for the germination of these evil acts? Would it not abolish apartheid, the seed of all evil in South Africa?

I was released after about four and a half hours, during which I denied being involved in any illegal activity of any sort, emphasized my love for change and peace, admitting ónly that "I told everything you did to me. Both in Europe and in the States."

Since then, some of our pastors have been visited, interrogated, and threatened, among them women pastors. Threats, intimidation, and fear of lingering death are our daily bread. In spite of perpetual denials by Pretoria that it is involved in homeland affairs, particularly in the so-called independent homelands, we, the victims of the ghosts of death, know that they are involved, not merely as secondary officials or advisers but as gods whose commands their black creatures follow with a loud amen. Mostly, the same team, black and white, that persecuted us in the past ten years and more continue, with a few additions, to harass us. Their methods are the same, their reasons are the same, and their goals are the same. In fact, the sophisticated torture station at Sibasa is situated in the white residential area, behind the same security fence that protects Pretoria's faithful. We not only know that the black police are mere puppets, we also see the strings and know who pulls them: they are as white as snow. This does not surprise us. Apartheid is the epitome of the divide-and-rule principle: use the "blacks" against "coloureds," and the "Indians" and "coloureds" against the "blacks," and "blacks" against "blacks," while the god of racism and ethnicity plays "father and peacemaker" from Pretoria.

Apartheid has ravaged our country. Many of our people have been forced to leave the country. Some are in prison. Many have been tortured, humiliated, and murdered. Many more will suffer the same fate as the God who is our friend, the friend of the oppressed in South Africa. Is God so greedy as not to share this friendship with others?

Let Us All Say No

We all say no to apartheid. The black community says no to apartheid. Many white people in South Africa say no to apartheid. The OAU says no to apartheid. The UN says no to apartheid. *Almighty God says no to the god of Pretoria.* In the name of the voiceless, the dead, the living, and the unborn, the confused, the tempted, and the misled, I join the world chorus: No to apartheid. For the sake of justice, human rights, and the equality of all South Africans, for the sake of the tortured, those who died under torture, those who are being tortured and who are now dying in detention as I write, and those who will still suffer and die under torture, I call upon humanity to shout at the top of her voice: NO to apartheid! In the name of human brotherhood and sisterhood, in the name of sense and logic, in the name of love and reconciliation, in the name of our descendants, *let us all say no to apartheid*. In God's name, apartheid is wrong, immoral, dangerous, and a threat to race relations, fellowship, reconciliation, and world peace. For how long shall the nations of the world pray,

> Our father who art in Pretoria
> Hallowed be thy gold
> Thy diamonds flow
> Thy will be done in the world as it is in Pretoria
> Give us this day our daily treasures
> And forgive us our pressures
> We promise not to forgive those who try to force us to pressure you
> Lead us not into abandoning you
> But deliver us from communism
> For thine is the policy of civilization
> of Western democracy
> and Christian standards
> For white, brown, and black?

EPILOGUE

JOHN A. EVENSON

In the weeks and months that followed Dean Farisani's release in 1982, concern for his health was uppermost in the minds of his family and co-workers. There was an understandable fear that the two heart attacks would leave permanent damage and that the beatings and electric-shock torture might have lasting effects. After spending some time at his home, he was sent by the church to a clinic near Cape Town for medical therapy, and then to West Germany. There he rested, and tried to regain his strength of mind as well as body. When we met in October 1982, he was still suffering from constant pain in his legs and a general state of weakness.

The reader must realize that Dean Farisani's release from prison was not the result of a change of attitude on the part of the South African authorities or their appointed black officials in Venda. Then, as now, the maintenance of white minority control was paramount. The government had, of course, no evidence that Dean Farisani had committed any crime, even under their apartheid legal system. They had not succeeded in silencing the dean through "suicide," and in spite of the torture they were unable to get Farisani to work for them. The South Africans were faced with a dilemma.

Through the work of Amnesty International around the world, Dean Farisani's case had become a cause célèbre. This important campaign was augmented by the concern of churches, especially the members of the Lutheran World Federation. Prayers for Dean Farisani and others in detention were offered regularly from churches and homes on six continents. Tremendous pressure from ordinary citizens was brought to bear on the governments of the United States, West Germany, and Great Britain. The South African embassies and Pretoria itself were besieged with letters protesting their actions in Venda. Pressure of this nature, especially since it came from the countries that have supported the South African government's program of gradual "reform," was counterproductive for Pretoria's interests. The white minority government relies on the United States, Great Britain, and West Germany to protect it from tough mandatory economic sanctions, so public opinion in those countries must be manipulated to achieve that support. One can surmise that the public-relations embarrassment regarding Dean Farisani outweighed the fear of his anti-apartheid voice in public once again. Farisani's release was not due to a conversion experience in Pretoria or in the security police headquarters in Sibasa but was an attempt at "damage control."

Perhaps the authorities thought that Dean Farisani would be content to return to his family and church and, with the reminder of his imprisonment, be more careful this time around. Others, clergy among them, had entered prison defiant, only to come out with a "new understanding." But the integrity of the man, with his love of God rather than fear of the authorities, resulted in a different scenario in Farisani's case.

While in West Germany, Dean Farisani rested and wrote the first draft of this book. He met with church leaders and congregations, traveling through West Germany, the Netherlands, the United States, and Scandinavia. During 1983–86 he made special trips on behalf of Amnesty International to parts of Africa, Europe, North America, Asia, and Oceania, providing a firsthand witness of the evil of apartheid, speaking on behalf of many others who would tell the story if only they could be heard. Inside South Africa, his sermons, his evangelistic messages, and his organizing activities continued as before: God's love did not permit people to be divided by the evil of apartheid.

After the medical leave, while still suffering from the pains of the torture, he returned to his parish and to the circuit. There were many broken relationships in need of healing, for some persons very close to the dean in the church had been "turned," by fear or other means, and used by the South Africans to spy on him and others, trying to trick them into revealing some imagined connections with banned organizations like the African National Congress. In some instances, repentance and forgiveness were shared. In others, no healing has taken place. One of those who took part in the torture sessions had been a lay leader in the church at Messina, assisting Dean Farisani with communion services. The congregation thought that he worked for the municipality. When the dean was arrested, the man was revealed as a plainclothes security policeman who actually told the guards to treat the dean cruelly. To this day he remains faithful to his masters in Pretoria.

In the northern Transvaal, the authorities continued to harass the dean, his family, and other pastors who had kept their faith. They were visited regularly by security police. "Freedom fighters" were sent to Farisani's home at night, looking for a "safe" place to stay. Regina or Simon would send them on their way, often seeing the same people during the next days in the friendly company of the security police. Threatening phone calls in the night, government cars trying to run them off the road, have become a regular feature of life for the Farisani family.

Dean Farisani and three others brought a civil action against the Venda authorities for their mistreatment during detention. Farisani received sixty-five hundred rand in damages. The government settled out of court. Thus Pretoria avoided the embarrassment of having its treatment of prisoners revealed in open session.

In February 1983, the two police officers present when Isaac Muofhe had been killed were acquitted of his murder by a three-man (white) court. It could not be proved, according to the judge, that Muofhe had been killed by the police, even though he had been in their charge at the time. In early 1986, a number of government officials calling themselves "members of the Lutheran church in Venda" wrote to Bishop Serote of the Northern Diocese, demanding that Dean Farisani and two other pastors be transferred out of Venda. The authorities again wanted to rid themselves of the meddlesome pastors and to force the Lutheran church to redefine its boundaries so that a "Venda Lutheran church" could be formed and controlled by the homeland government.

Bishop Serote had stood fast through the detentions of Dean Farisani and other pastors, doing his best to bring about their release in a situation where one could not always count on the support of other church leaders. Serote stood firm again, writing a letter to all the congregations and church workers in the circuit, telling them, "We have long gone beyond the stage where we can be manipulated by individuals for personal or ethnic interests." There had been a time, he reminded them, when Dean Farisani and other pastors "were taken away from you and made to suffer for things they were never found guilty of. Your loyalty and steadfastness in those days is remembered with pride." Serote refused to transfer the pastors, and the government backed down.

Late at night on November 21, 1986, the security police surrounded the Farisani home. The dean and his family barricaded themselves in their bedroom and used the telephone to alert friends that they were under siege. At six o'clock in the morning, November 22, Dean Farisani gave himself up and was taken into custody once again. At the police station, he was faced with the same group of interrogators who had almost tortured him to death in 1982. He refused to talk to them and demanded to be released. The dean knew that if these men tortured him again, they would never let him out alive.

Once more the word went out through the network of Amnesty International and the Lutheran World Federation. Representatives from Amnesty and the Berlin Mission Society were dispatched to Sibasa to demand Farisani's release.

In January 1987, the dean was able to get a message out of prison to his family and bishop. In the letter, dated January 7, Farisani said that he had started a hunger strike on January 1, vowing not to eat until he was released or charged with a crime. The dean said that his life had been threatened by the interrogator who tortured him during a previous period of detention, who said, "We shall close your mouth once and for all." Addressed to his wife, the letter included a will. "I suspect," he wrote, "that this is a revenge detention for exposing my previous tortures to the world, for my stand against apartheid. . . ." The letter was signed "your loving husband in a dungeon of cruelty."

Again the eyes of the world focused on South Africa's "independent homeland" of Venda. The letters, telegrams, and news articles started. International pressure mounted. On January 30, Dean Farisani was released. The United States Department of State later reported that it had received twenty-six thousand messages protesting Farisani's imprisonment.

This detention, Dean Farisani was not physically tortured, but there were threats against his life, and the interrogation periods were more intense than in all previous imprisonments combined. Weak from the hunger strike and the psychological pressures of interrogation, he was sent by Bishop Serote for treatment at a clinic near Johannesburg.

In February, Farisani received word from the South African government that his right to travel in the Republic of South Africa had been revoked. He was, in effect, imprisoned in Venda. The banning order made it impossible to receive treatment in South Africa.

Under the banning order, Farisani may not enter any part of white South Africa without the permission of the Pretoria government. Venda is itself divided into three parts, with "white" South Africa coming in between. He would thus need a visa to visit his mother in another part of the Bantustan. Since Venda is completely surrounded by South Africa and has no commercial airport, the dean needed special permission to travel abroad.

But the effect of the banning order on his pastoral work is the most far-reaching of all. His circuit covers three hundred square kilometers (116 square miles), with 121 congregations in Venda, "white" South Africa, and parts of two other Bantustans. The restriction cuts him off from half of his parishioners. He cannot, for example, visit his congregation at Beit Bridge, on the border with Zimbabwe. And as deputy bishop for the Northern Diocese, he must also assist bishops on other circuits.

Farisani's work on the diaconate and human-rights committees for the whole circuit will also be seriously hindered. Farisani is also a member of the church council of the Evangelical Lutheran Church in South Africa, which holds regular meetings in Johannesburg. He was unable to attend such a meeting in February.

He decided to seek medical treatment in the United States. With the help of pressure from Western governments and the church he was granted a special twelve-hour transit visa to drive the six hundred kilometers from his home in Sibasa to the airport at Johannesburg. Since the visa was granted at the last minute (only six hours remained until take-off), he was forced to drive at speeds of up to 180 kilometers per hour in order to catch the London flight.

Farisani proceeded to the United States. He is receiving medical treatment with his family at the Center for Torture Victims in St. Paul, Minnesota. Making it clear that he has not "gone into exile," Farisani says he will return to South Africa to continue his work as a pastor and dean of the Evangelical Lutheran Church in Southern Africa. Bishop Serote and the church lawyers are working to overturn the travel restrictions. The dean is preparing to return to South Africa to continue his ministry, but the white men still rule in Pretoria.

April 13, 1987